MADE TO BELONG

MADE TO BELONG

A 6-WEEK JOURNEY TO DISCOVER
YOUR LIFE'S PURPOSE

Rachel Anne Ridge

BELONG tour

TYNDALE®
MOMENTUM

An Imprint of
Tyndale House Publishers, Inc.

Visit The BELONG Tour at www.BELONGtour.com.

Visit Tyndale online at www.tyndale.com.

Visit Tyndale Momentum online at www.tyndalemomentum.com.

Tyndale Momentum and the Tyndale Momentum logo are registered trademarks of Tyndale House Publishers, Inc. Tyndale Momentum is an imprint of Tyndale House Publishers, Inc., Carol Stream, Illinois.

Made to Belong: A 6-Week Journey to Discover Your Life's Purpose

Designed by Kristin Bakken

Edited by Bonne Steffen and Susan Ellingburg. Executive Editor, Leslie Nunn Reed.

ISBN 978-1-4964-0836-5

Printed in the United States of America

22	21	20	19	18	17	16
7	6	5	4	3	2	1

To you, dear reader.

Start where you are.

You're right where you're supposed to be.

CONTENTS

INTRODUCTION

IN MY PREVIOUS CAREER as a professional artist, the very hardest part of every painting was the perfectly terrifying moment of standing in front of a blank canvas, *before I'd even begun.*

Paintbrushes in hand, supplies at the ready, sketch neatly taped to a nearby wall.

A clock ticking loudly in my head.

"Hooo. Hooo-boy."

After a big exhale, I'd close my eyes and try to pull my creative thoughts together.

Man, I'm thirsty! I'd leave to get a glass of water.

I'd walk by the computer. *Hmmm, I'd better check my e-mail.*

Finally, I'd step back in front of the canvas.

Okay.

Wait, why is this tag in my shirt so scratchy? I need to change my shirt.

Better. Back in the studio, back in position.

The white, intimidating expanse of stretched canvas would glare at me, silently taunting.

"You can't do this."

"You don't know where to start."

"You're not qualified."

"You will mess up."

"You are too old for this."

"Other artists could do a better job."

"You have no talent."

"You will fail."

I'm not making this up. This is actually what blank canvases say. They sort of narrow their eyes and lean back on their easels, just *daring* you to throw a blob of paint on them. They're very haughty that way.

Thankfully, this is where an *underpainting* comes in.

Underpainting, you ask?

Master artists will tell you that the underpainting is a light, loose layer of paint that roughs in the composition of what will later become the final painting. Often done with shades of one color, its purpose is to give the artist a chance to see the design on the canvas easily and quickly, without getting stuck in the details.

I call an underpainting a psychological kick in the pants to get started. You see, an underpainting isn't supposed to be perfect. It isn't supposed to be the final product. It isn't even supposed to be pretty. It is simply a guide that will be corrected, covered up, and finessed, and will ultimately become a masterpiece.

An underpainting doesn't worry about getting it right the first time.

Its purpose is to be built upon.

To give structure.

To be painted over.

To help the artist see where she could go, and what corrections she might need to make along the way.

Underpaintings often don't even resemble the finished art piece, because somewhere in between the first broad strokes of loose color and the final layering of fine detail, the painting changes. It becomes infused with excitement and color, and gradually comes alive as a vibrant work of art.

Underpaintings help the artist know where—and how—to begin.

In our six weeks together, we are going to be talking about a big subject: purpose.

The idea of finding your life purpose can be as intimidating as all get-out.

I mean, where do you even begin on that intimidating blank canvas in front of you?

Maybe you feel stuck where you are, and you don't know where to start to discover your purpose.

Maybe you have a sense that you are called to something important, something bigger than what you're doing, but you just don't know what that thing actually is.

Maybe you've got a spark of dream but don't know what to do with it.

Perhaps you already know your purpose, but it doesn't seem to have anything to do with what's happening in your life right now.

Maybe you've been waiting and waiting for circumstances to change so you can pursue your calling.

It could be that the voices in your head have been talking to the blank-canvas voices in my studio, and they're telling you, in their raspy little tones,

"You don't have a purpose."

"You don't know where to start."

"You're too old."

"God can't use you."

"You have no talent."

"Your abilities are too small."

"Your dream is silly."

"You will fail."

And you're standing there, gulping for air and hoping for inspiration.

Let me tell you:

You're exactly where you're supposed to be right now.

I believe with all my heart that if you are reading this book, you are already knee-deep in the river of God's purpose for your life. It is no accident that this book is in your hands.

In this study, we'll spend some time in a small, little-known book of the Bible that will spark our imaginations. We'll ask questions, try some new things, and step out of our comfort zones. We'll even have a bit of fun while we're doing it, because there is *joy in discovery*. I believe that God takes delight in us, and it brings Him pleasure to watch us grow and become all that we can be.

Together, we will throw some paint on the canvas. Hand in hand, we will make small steps toward something great. We will create some structure and develop a composition that will put you on a path toward understanding your purpose and calling.

We aren't going to worry about creating a perfect masterpiece here.

We are going to call this our messy underpainting.

Because our job is simply to begin.

We'll leave the final brushstrokes to God.

What do you say? Are you with me?

Let's get started.

Week One
PURPOSED BY GOD

. . . .

*Purpose (n): the reason for which something is done
or created or for which something exists.*
GOOGLE DICTIONARY

MOST OF US HAVE A FEELING deep down inside that we were made for something more. At least, we hope there is a specific purpose for our lives! You know, some kind of grand design. Then we look at the activities that fill our days and wonder just what kind of specific purpose could be found in all of this.

Life seems to be filled to the brim with busyness. Between work, family obligations, raising kids, community involvement, and maintaining the "stuff" of life (like remembering to change the oil in your car and taking out the trash), it can feel more like a long list of tasks than a purpose-filled trajectory toward a big calling. But somewhere in the midst of the deadlines and car pools we sense a longing to know the reason we were created, the reason we are here.

That desire for "something more" is innately human and unique to our consciousness.

In the short chapters of this book, I'd like to suggest that the search for purpose must begin with the understanding that God has created us this way. He wants us to experience this longing! Rather than feeling sad about the longing, let's take a moment and savor the idea that the desire to know His purpose puts us squarely in God's sweet spot.

He is absolutely pleased with our search.

Have you ever thought about it this way? In Ecclesiastes—a book of collected wisdom from one of the wisest men in history—chapter 3, verse 11 says that God has placed eternity in our human hearts, and only the recognition of something much bigger than ourselves—something eternal—will satisfy us. He's wired each of us in unique ways, given us special hopes and dreams, and provided us with skills and abilities so that we can be part of His ongoing creation and work in this world.

That stirring in your soul? That's God's incredible invitation to participate.

.... *Day One* ....

MADE IN AND THROUGH

. . . .

"For as the waters fill the sea, the earth will be filled with an awareness of the glory of God."

HABAKKUK 2:14

IN THE NEXT SIX WEEKS we'll explore the short Old Testament book of Habakkuk together. As we do, I want you to keep something in mind: God is a brilliant multitasker. At any given time, His purposes are always at work in your life, and they unfold in two distinct ways:

1. God's purpose for *every person*. This has to do with *who you are*: your character, your spiritual life, and your connectedness to others. It is all about your heart.

2. God's unique, overarching purpose for you in the ways your experiences, your personality, your gifts, and your unique wiring work together. This has to do with *what you do*: you could say it's all about your hands.

Now, it's tempting to leapfrog over number one (who you are) and go straight to number two (what you do), but you might miss something big if you do. The fact of the matter is, *who you are is far more important to God than what you do.* As far as He is concerned, no grand purpose in the world can ever replace a heart that wants to know and love Him, and to that end He will always be working, through every circumstance, to help you find Him and experience His love. Simply put,

God is working in you, so that He can work through you.

Even if you don't know what the "through you" part is going to look like, it's exciting to know that the "in you" part is already under way! As a person placed on this planet, you are loved beyond measure and treasured more than you can imagine. God is filling you with His character and grace, His mercy and wisdom, and His life and peace. He is empowering you to take on bold new dreams and to dare to believe that He has something more for you than a life filled with tasks and activities. His current work within your heart reveals that God is cooking up something good! He has a vision and a purpose for your life—not just for the future, but even for today.

God's purpose for your life is not an assignment to complete, but an invitation to participate.

This week, we'll park at purpose number one: God's purpose for everyone.

READ

God is working in you, giving you the desire and the power to do what pleases him. PHILIPPIANS 2:13

The Lord—who is the Spirit—makes us more and more like him as we are changed into his glorious image.
2 CORINTHIANS 3:18

I am certain that God, who began the good work within you, will continue his work until it is finally finished on the day when Christ Jesus returns.   PHILIPPIANS 1:6

REFLECT

Take a moment to consider how God's purpose is already at work in you. Think or meditate on the verses above, and thank Him for His power and love revealed in your life.

RESPOND

1. Name three positive characteristics your *present circumstances* are producing in your life: _____

    _____

    _____

    _____

    _____

    _____

2. What is one way you are becoming more mature in your thoughts or actions?   _____

    _____

    _____

    _____

    _____

    _____

3. Galatians 5:22-23 lists the fruit of the Spirit: love, joy, peace, patience, kindness, goodness, faithfulness, gentleness, and self-control. Today, do one out-of-the-box activity that demonstrates one of these characteristics. Go ahead, make a bold statement with your actions!

Today, I will demonstrate _____ by

_____

_____

_____

_____

_____

Here is what happened as a result of my "fruit of the Spirit" action: _____

_____

_____

_____

_____

_____

_____

_____

_____

Day Two
MADE TO BE LOVED

"O LORD my God, my Holy One . . ."

HABAKKUK 1:12

I REMEMBER THE FIRST women's retreat I ever attended. I'd left a toddler and a barely weaned baby at home with my husband and was eager to make new friends with my cabinmates. The previous two years had brought a huge change in my "job description," and I was struggling to find my footing as a stay-at-home mom. The other ladies, most of them older than I, lounged on their cots or sat cross-legged on sleeping bags as we began our small group time. One by one, each of them introduced herself to the group and told us about her life. They seemed so confident, so polished, so self-assured. They described their jobs, their car pools, their homeschooling, their hobbies. As my turn approached, I could feel tears welling up behind my eyes.

I could think of nothing interesting to say about myself.

After all, my days were spent nursing a baby, changing diapers, and chasing a toddler. I barely ever got out of the house, and when I did I always had baby spit-up on my shoulders.

Finally, all eyes were upon me.

I sputtered, "My name is Rachel . . . and I make my bed every day." That was it.

That was all I could say that I accomplished on a regular basis. Much to my horror, a couple of those tears escaped and trickled down my cheek.

"Oh, honey!" The women encircled me. "You're a *mama!*"

"Mothering little ones is hard work! It takes a lot of love and sacrifice."

"You're doing something really important."

"I never managed to make my bed when my kids were little," one of them said with a laugh, and suddenly I felt like I was Woman of the Year.

That day, the women in the circle showed me that "accomplishments" were not a true measure of my worth. They affirmed me in ways that went far deeper than how many stacks of clean clothes I'd put away or how perfect my home looked. They made me feel loved. They welcomed me into their lives without first doing a spot check to see if I met a list of standards. In a small way, they reflected what God does for each of us.

Hooray! God's not checking my laundry baskets.

In all seriousness, God's not holding up impossible standards for us to keep before He showers us with His love. There's no prerequisite for His acceptance of us. There's no checklist for us to do first. This is really important to know because sometimes we get a little confused about things, thinking we have to fulfill a grand purpose *in order for* Him to love us.

God's love is purely unconditional.

It's not tied to our performance or our accomplishments. It does not rest on how well we do on some test. It is all based on His grace for us.

That's tough to accept in our modern, achievement-oriented world. We've been trained to work for the A+, for the promotions, for the attaboys . . . by trying harder and doing more. We are conditioned to believe in a merit system that says, "You must earn your way."

God's grace, by contrast, says, "You are enough."

"You are enough for Me to love, to sacrifice for, and to invite you to be with Me forever."

Just as you are.

READ

God saved you by his grace when you believed. And you can't take credit for this; it is a gift from God. Salvation is not a reward for the good things we have done, so none of us can boast about it. EPHESIANS 2:8-9

I am convinced that nothing can ever separate us from God's love. Neither death nor life, neither angels nor demons, neither our fears for today nor our worries about tomorrow—not even the powers of hell can separate us from God's love. No power in the sky above or in the earth below—indeed, nothing in all creation will ever be able to separate us from the love of God that is revealed in Christ Jesus our Lord. ROMANS 8:38-39

REFLECT

The honest truth, please:

Do you ever feel like you need to earn God's love or approval? ___

_____

_____

How does this affect the way you approach God? _____

_____

_____

_____

_____

How does this affect the way you think about your purpose? _____

_____

_____

_____

_____

_____

RESPOND

Find a quiet place to spend a few moments alone. Think about the following:

1. What would it feel like to be completely known—every thought, every action, every mistake, every doubt, hope, fear, and dream—and *to be completely accepted*? _____

   _____

   _____

   _____

   _____

   _____

2. Imagine undergoing a complete scan of your mind and self— all the secrets inside revealed—and as each part of you was scanned, it was deemed precious, accepted, and worthy of love. How would you respond? _____

   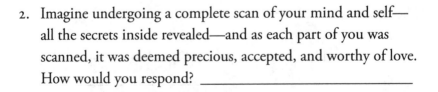

_____

_____

_____

_____

_____

3. What if you felt no shame for anything in your past or
   anything in your present life, and felt no fear about the future?
   How would it affect your decisions? Your relationships? Your
   current situation? _____

   _____

   _____

   _____

   _____

   _____

This is what God's grace is: Total acceptance. Total love. Rest in that
for a moment. In fact, rest in it all week.

How does it change the way you see yourself? _____

_____

_____

_____

_____

_____

_____

Write out the following verse and put it where you can see it every day.

I am convinced that nothing can ever separate us from
God's love. Neither death nor life, neither angels nor
demons, neither our fears for today nor our worries about
tomorrow—not even the powers of hell can separate us

from God's love. No power in the sky above or in the earth below—indeed, nothing in all creation will ever be able to separate us from the love of God that is revealed in Christ Jesus our Lord.   ROMANS 8:38-39

.... *Day Three* ....
MADE TO BELONG

· ·

*"God's brilliant splendor fills the heavens, and the earth
is filled with his praise."*

HABAKKUK 3:1

As a child, I loved our family Christmas traditions. Because we are descendants of Norwegian immigrants, our holiday activities had a distinctively Scandinavian flavor. Christmas Eve was our big event, beginning with a sumptuous candlelit dinner on the best china. There was always a selection of Norwegian goodies, like *lefse*, a tortilla-like flatbread made from potatoes, and cookies and sweets made from recipes handed down through the generations. Unfortunately, no Christmas dinner was complete without a plate of boiled codfish called *lutefisk*, which smelled just as awful as it tasted. How anyone actually liked it is still a huge mystery to me, but it was our ethnic tradition, and so we suffered on.

The family gift exchange could not take place until the dishes were done (which seemed to take forever) and after everyone settled in the living room for a short program by the children, which included the reading of the Christmas story from the Bible. It was a near-magical night, something that was unique and special to us.

As a family, we belong to each other, and not just through shared traditions. We are marked by a shared history, shared responsibilities, shared privileges, and most of all, a shared love for one another. It's really no surprise that God uses the concept of family when describing the people who follow Him. When you choose to enter into a relationship with Jesus, the Bible says you are adopted into God's family, and you're given all the shared privileges and responsibilities of a daughter or son (Romans 8:15-17, 22-24). What an exceptional gift.

It's within this context of family that purpose begins to take shape.

There is a distinctiveness to being part of one big family. There is a belongingness, a shared history, a common ground. We are connected to each other, even when we are separated by physical miles.

Not only does God use the word *family* to describe us (Ephesians 2:19), but He also uses the word *body* (1 Corinthians 12:12). It's the idea that we are all important parts of one whole. Each one of us needs the others in order to fully function. Just as an eye can't say to a hand, "I don't need you," and the head can't say to the feet, "I don't need you" (1 Corinthians 12:19-21), it's the same with this body of people who follow Jesus. We need one another. You and I are necessary for the health of the entire unit.

And here's the thing: as both a body and a family, we are marked not by human genetics, but by love for each other. God's love imprints on us, and it becomes the basis for all that we do. It's this love that makes us different from the world. It's this love that motivates us to learn and grow, and to reach out to others. It's how we know God's Spirit is with us.

Love is the only thing that the Bible calls the "greatest" thing (1 Corinthians 13:13), and John 13:34-35 says, "Now I am giving you a new commandment: Love each other. Just as I have loved you, you should love each other. Your love for one another will prove to the world that you are my disciples."

READ

Now you Gentiles are no longer strangers and foreigners. You are citizens along with all of God's holy people. You are members of God's family. EPHESIANS 2:19

See how very much our Father loves us, for he calls us his children, and that is what we are! 1 JOHN 3:1

Dear friends, let us continue to love one another, for love comes from God. Anyone who loves is a child of God and knows God. But anyone who does not love does not know God, for God is love. 1 JOHN 4:7-8

Is there any encouragement from belonging to Christ? Any comfort from his love? Any fellowship together in the Spirit? Are your hearts tender and compassionate? Then make me truly happy by agreeing wholeheartedly with each other, loving one another, and working together with one mind and purpose. Don't be selfish; don't try to impress others. Be humble, thinking of others as better than yourselves. Don't look out only for your own interests, but take an interest in others, too. You must have the same attitude that Christ Jesus had. PHILIPPIANS 2:1-5

Just as our bodies have many parts and each part has a special function, so it is with Christ's body. We are many parts of one body, and we all belong to each other.   ROMANS 12:4-5

REFLECT

God chose to use the terms *family* and *body* for His followers. Do you feel a part of this family? _____

_____

God's purpose for you starts within this family. He gives gifts and abilities to each person in order for the whole body to function. What gifts and abilities do you have, and what roles and responsibilities do you fill? _____

_____

What rights and privileges do you think come with membership in this kind of family? _____

_____

What does being part of a family mean to you? _____

_____

_____

RESPOND

1. If being part of a family is one of God's purposes for every person who follows Him, how is that reflected in your life? Are you connected to others in a deep relational way? Do you feel needed? Why or why not? _____

    _____

    _____

_____

_____

_____

2. Describe your role (or what you'd like your role to be) in a family of people. This could be a local church, a group of friends, or even the study group using this workbook._____

_____

_____

_____

_____

_____

_____

3. In what ways do you rely on others? _____

_____

_____

_____

_____

_____

_____

4. Being part of a family requires a level of unselfishness to make it work. Describe a time when you unselfishly served another person or group, and what it felt like. _____

_____

_____

_____

_____

_____

5. As in every family, there may be things you would like to change but feel you can't (like our Norwegian *lutefisk*). Are you bound by other people's expectations to remain the same, or do you have freedom to make changes—in roles, traditions, beliefs, activities? Why or why not?_____

_____

_____

_____

_____

_____

_____

.... Day Four ....
MADE TO GROW

. . . .

"Look and be amazed . . ."
HABAKKUK 1:5

WHEN I WAS IN COLLEGE, one of my professors was known around campus for her extensive wardrobe. Every day she wore a different outfit to class, with perfectly matching accessories, and every day I sat in awe. I couldn't tear my eyes away from her. She was a fashion plate from head to toe, and it was mesmerizing.

Unfortunately, her wardrobe was from 1969 . . . and it was now the mid-1980s. Each outfit, from the plaid bell-bottom pantsuits, to the pleated skirts with knee socks and loafers, to the silky blouses tied at the waist, made her look as if she'd stepped off the pages of *Vogue*— fifteen years earlier. Walking into her classroom was like being in a time warp. I had to touch my eighties perm and adjust my shoulder pads to remember that I was in the right decade! Thankfully, I had a Rubik's Cube in my slouchy purse to keep me grounded.

My teacher's outdated fashion sense was the subject of a few snickers from the back of the room, although perhaps she showed more sense than the rest of us by not embracing the eighties. Nonetheless, the memory reminds me how easy it is to get stuck in one place and never learn to embrace change or growth.

Getting stuck happens all the time, most often when we find something that seems to work well for a season. I mean, my college instructor's style was *darling*. But she didn't realize that she'd "aged out" of the outfits from her sorority days. When I looked closely, the seams were stretched a little tight, and the fabric was worn. And the clothes were simply out of date. For us, maybe it's a set of beliefs, or a way of dealing with problems, or a habit that provides relief to our stressed-out lives that is wearing thin. But our go-to strategy becomes so familiar and comfortable that we don't even realize when it's not working anymore. We miss the fact that it's time to move on, or make new choices, or grow up.

The thing is . . . we were made to grow.

If we aren't growing spiritually and emotionally, we're short-changing ourselves and others around us. We can't fulfill any purpose or reach our dreams at all. The great news is that flourishing in God's purpose for our lives means that we'll always be growing. It's that aspect of God working "in you" that we talked about in day one. It is present and ongoing because God is always working on our hearts. His work will never go out of style or be outgrown.

Remember the little book of Habakkuk I mentioned? It reads a bit like a journal, showing how the writer grows in understanding and maturity as time and events move along.

Habakkuk starts with a complaint.

But he ends by giving praise and thanks to God.

And in between? There are questions, and preparation, and change. There is learning, and there is growth. Within Habakkuk's lines, we see character qualities emerge that remind us that this is how God's purpose works in us as He is working through us.

READ

Habakkuk chapters 1–3

Today's reading is an entire book of the Bible, but it's a short read. I want you to get a flavor of what the book is about, since it provides the backdrop to our study.

REFLECT

As you read the chapters, look for the progression of growth that takes place in Habakkuk. Here is an outline to help you.

1. Habakkuk's first complaint: 1:1-4

2. God's first answer: 1:5-11

3. Habakkuk's second complaint: 1:12–2:1

4. God's second answer: 2:2-20

5. Habakkuk's prayer-like song: 3:1-19

RESPOND

Like Habakkuk, we are called to grow—spiritually, mentally, and emotionally. Sometimes the most difficult situations we face bring about the most growth. What are some situations you've faced that have caused you to grow? _____

_____

_____

_____

_____

_____

.... Day Five ....
MADE FOR AUTHENTICITY

"How long, O LORD, must I call for help?"

HABAKKUK 1:2

HAVE YOU EVER ENCOUNTERED someone for the first time and, without knowing anything about her, instantly liked her?

Maybe there was something in the woman's voice that made you feel good, or you found her facial expression to be interesting or engaging. Perhaps there was something about her sense of style that made you take notice.

Or maybe you found yourselves in a shared situation, like experiencing terrible service in a restaurant, and you caught each other's exasperated eyes from over your tables. You didn't know anything about her background, her family, her story, or what was wrong with her order, but you connected immediately. And when you heard her ask to speak to the manager, you knew you were born to be soul sisters.

This is my kind of person, you think. *Someone who speaks her mind.*

Well, that's just how I feel about the obscure man we met yesterday in the pages of the Bible's Old Testament. The encounter is brief—just three short chapters in the middle part of the Bible where the pages sometimes get stuck together and you can miss an entire book with a flip of a page clump. In this section there's a handful of books collectively known as the Minor Prophets because they are so short. The chapters in this particular book don't seem to be long enough for us to get to know the author well, but somehow he leaves an impression.

This is our kind of guy.

We know his name: Habakkuk. (I know, right? What was his mother thinking?) We also know his occupation: he was a prophet, and most scholars believe he was also a musician in the Temple, which is where he made his home. His job as a prophet was important to the people of his day, because Bibles didn't exist at that time. God used prophets like Habakkuk to communicate to them what was on His heart.

You might be familiar with Daniel (of the lions' den account), who was a contemporary of Habakkuk. But this man gets a lot less space in the Bible. We don't know a whole lot about him, but that's okay because we like him already.

He opens with revealing honesty. It's a complaint. And he's going straight to management with it: "How long, O Lord, must I call for help?"

Hey, he's just saying what everyone else is thinking.

How long, O Lord, are you going to wait to answer me?

Digging in with resolve, Habakkuk stands out among his fellow prophets, who delivered God's message without much commentary and certainly without direct complaint to the Almighty. Few people in that day had that kind of audacity. The honesty and humanity with which Habakkuk talks to God tells us something about him that we can relate to. He's exasperated, and he's not afraid to voice it.

But Habakkuk doesn't stop there, and this is why I admire him so much. In the verses that follow he reveals a heart that is open and a willingness to listen. He is authentic, through and through.

Habakkuk speaks his mind, then positions himself to hear and respond.

Like us, Habakkuk is waiting on a vision.

He knows he needs to hear from God. He needs a message that will give him direction and clarity. He is looking for an answer that will make a difference in the world around him.

This interaction between Habakkuk and God will provide the basis for the rest of our underpainting in this study. We will reference Habakkuk's story to help us discover God's purpose for our lives, finding ways to draw modern life principles for ourselves from this ancient conversation.

There is gold here, my friend.

So let's begin with authenticity, just as Habakkuk does.

READ

This is the message that the prophet Habakkuk received
in a vision.
How long, O LORD, must I call for help?

HABAKKUK 1:1-2

I am sick at heart.
How long, O LORD, until you restore me?

PSALM 6:3

In my distress I cried out to the LORD;
yes, I prayed to my God for help.
He heard me from his sanctuary;
my cry to him reached his ears.

PSALM 18:6

REFLECT

Be honest: Have you ever cried out, "How long, O Lord?" I sure have.

- How long will I have to wait?
- How long will I have to work at this job that seems to suck the life from me?
- How long until I understand my purpose and calling?
- How long will it take until I know what I'm "supposed to do" when I grow up?
- How long until I can go "pro" in my calling and really live fully?

Here's the thing: God invites our honest, heartfelt cries. He doesn't mind when we express our exasperation and frustration. In fact, He invites it. So we might as well get real. If you're waiting on a vision or calling, wondering what your purpose is or how to get there, let Him know how you feel. Go ahead—He won't mind.

RESPOND

What is your "How long, O Lord?" prayer today? What is it that you are waiting on? Write it on the following lines or use the prayer that I've included on the next page as a place to start. _____

_____

_____

_____

_____

_____

_____

Dear God, sometimes it feels like I'll never discover my purpose. It feels like it's taking forever for You to answer my prayer for guidance and help. I want to understand Your plan and find peace in the knowledge that You hear me. Take my discouragement and frustration and replace it with faith and joy. Help me to trust You with all my concerns and allow You to fill me with confidence that You are with me on this journey. Amen.

Week Two
PREPARED TO ASK QUESTIONS

. . . .

"Have patience with everything unresolved in your heart. . . .
Live the questions now. Perhaps . . . you will gradually,
without even noticing it, live your way into the answer."

RAINER MARIA RILKE

WHO? WHAT? WHERE? WHEN? WHY? Remember those questions from
your high school English class? This week, we are going to take our
cue from Habakkuk's first four verses, in which he presents the five
Ws to set the stage for the rest of his book. It's a great literary move,
one my tenth-grade teacher would applaud, because it provides context for the message. In a similar way, the five Ws are a perfect vehicle
to give context to our study's theme of purpose. We'll ask ourselves
questions pertaining to our hopes, dreams, experiences, and passions,
and we'll let the answers simmer from here on out. As we make our
way through each day's reading and application, I want you to keep
in mind two things:

1. *Begin with an underpainting.* Don't let perfectionism keep you
   from "throwing paint on the canvas." Answer the questions and

fill in the blanks without worrying about making it pretty, or about what someone might think. Remember, you are *roughing in* a framework for the rest of the painting, not trying to get it right the first time.

2. *Know you are loved.* Your hopes and dreams, your disappointments and failures, your highs and lows—they are all held tenderly in the arms of God. I encourage you to stay in that space of trust. It can be difficult to open up areas that are sensitive, that may cause you to wince when peeling back the layers of the past. That's okay. Simply take your time and let His Spirit lead you gently. He wants to create something beautiful here, and He wants to redeem all things for His glory and grace.

Day One
WHO DO YOU WANT TO BE?

"This is the message that the prophet Habakkuk received in a vision."

HABAKKUK 1:1

My husband, Tom, and I have been married for more than thirty years. For the last fifteen, we've worked together, so we know each other *pretty* well. Tom is an interesting guy, an outdoorsman who loves hunting and fishing, backpacking and camping. He is more at home in a pair of waders and a camouflage shirt than in a coat and tie. When he's not busy outside or coaching hockey, he loves to read about science and theology, as well as catching up with the sports page. After so many years together, I believe I've reached "expert status" in what makes him tick.

One evening, I was hard at work trying to find just the right piece of music for a slide show I was preparing, while Tom was busy with some of his own paperwork at a nearby table. I played song after song on my phone, using a free music streaming app. I tried a classical piece: Vivaldi's *Four Seasons*. Nope, not quite right. A jazzy one? Not right either. How about a piece from a film score? *Pride and Prejudice*! That's just the ticket! In triumph I turned up the volume and played the beautiful theme "Mrs. Darcy" written by Dario Marianelli and featuring pianist Jean-Yves Thibaudet.

Without missing a beat, Tom looked up and said in a perfect British accent, "You have bewitched me body and soul," then turned back to his work. Like it was *perfectly normal* for an outdoorsman/sports guy to be quoting a Jane Austen movie.

Well, I about fell off my chair. "Do I even know who you are?" I sputtered.

He looked at me and shrugged, as if to say, "I don't know. Do you?"

I could not stop laughing all evening, tickled at the sheer unexpectedness of my husband's nonchalant but well-timed quip.

To be honest, I don't know if *he* even knew that he knew that beautiful line from Mr. Darcy. But it had surfaced from all the times he'd made a point to sit and watch our daughters' favorite movie with them. You see, long before then, he'd decided that he wanted to be that dad, the one who learned details that were important to his girls. The one who would notice his daughters' hairstyles and take an interest in their favorite bands. The one who would make popcorn for everyone, watch Jane Austen movies, and learn things about the characters.

Tom had decided who he wanted to be . . . and it showed up in surprising ways. His Mr. Darcy moment was a natural outflow of an inward change he'd embraced years before.

Who do you want to be?

It's a question we rarely ask ourselves, perhaps because we are afraid we'll have to live up to our own "impossible" standards. Or maybe because once we realized we'd never become president, or a professional ballerina, or an astronaut, we decided it was useless to set a goal for ourselves. And so we muddle through life without a clear vision of the person we want to be.

Habakkuk, on the other hand, was clear about who he was. With a bold stroke, he signed his name to his vision and added "the prophet" to his signature. He knew who he was and why he was on earth: to hear God's message and to tell the people what he heard. It wasn't just a job description; it was a lifestyle. It required personal sacrifice and comfort. Dedication and perseverance. Focus and commitment. You didn't get to be a prophet of his day by muddling through life. He found his calling and then did what it took to live it.

So, who do you want to be? Let's spend some time writing things down. Don't worry about the seeming impossibility of your dream. Simply allow yourself to think big, imagine creatively, and live boldly on the page.

READ

Thank you for making me so wonderfully complex!
　　Your workmanship is marvelous—how well I know it.
PSALM 139:14

Delight yourself in the LORD,
　　and he will give you the desires of your heart.
PSALM 37:4, ESV

Keep on asking, and you will receive what you ask for. Keep on seeking, and you will find. Keep on knocking, and the door will be opened to you. For everyone who asks, receives. Everyone who seeks, finds. And to everyone who knocks, the door will be opened. MATTHEW 7:7-8

REFLECT

Imagine that you are writing a book or a movie script of your ideal life. What would your character look like? What would she do for a living? How would she respond to obstacles and setbacks? How would she respond to success? I find that I have to "turn off" the voice in my head that tells me this is an unrealistic or unproductive activity. Remember there are no right or wrong answers; we are just letting our imaginations stretch.

RESPOND

1. Write your character sketch on the following lines. _____
    _____
    _____
    _____
    _____
    _____

2. What are some habits or qualities of your ideal person that you don't currently have? (For example, my ideal character gets out of bed early and exercises.)_____
    _____
    _____
    _____
    _____
    _____

3. What are some habits or qualities of your ideal person that you do have already? _____
    _____
    _____
    _____

_____

_____

4. What are some of the things you feel pressured from outside
   sources to do or be? Why do you feel this pressure? _____

   _____

   _____

   _____

   _____

   _____

5. Name someone whom you admire. What is it about that
   person that makes you admire him or her? _____

   _____

   _____

   _____

   _____

   _____

6. If failure was not a possible outcome, what would you choose
   to do? _____

   _____

   _____

   _____

   _____

7. Create a goal statement by answering this question in one
   or two sentences: _Who do I want to become?_ _____

   _____

   _____

   _____

   _____

.... *Day Two* ....
WHAT BURDENS YOU?

. . . .

"Wherever I look, I see destruction and violence."

HABAKKUK 1:3

MY FRIEND PRISCILLA AND I like going to movies together. We usually pick lighthearted "chick flicks" that we know would bore our husbands to death, so we spare them the pain and suffering. Isn't that just so *unselfish* of us?

One night Priscilla and I chose a sappy romantic movie. There we sat with our popcorn and sodas, pulled into the beautiful love story filled with twists and turns. And then . . . the lead male character died! I couldn't believe it. *No! All the happiness they could have had together, all the joy, all the love. It can't be. Please come back! Why didn't I read the reviews before buying a ticket?*

As the screen faded to black, the music swelled, and the credits started to roll, Priscilla turned to me.

"Well, that movie didn't do a *thing* for me," she said, dry-eyed and bored, brushing popcorn crumbs from her shirt.

"Me either," I sobbed. Tears streamed down my face as I blew my nose into a napkin. "Not a thing."

Priscilla leaned forward and squinted at me through the darkness. "Rachel, are you *crying*?"

"Maybe a little," I managed to choke out. "Just give me a minute to pull myself together."

She stared at me in disbelief, then finally asked, "Did we see the same movie?"

We've laughed about that night for years. But it raises an interesting question: How is it possible for two people to see the exact same thing, at the same time, and yet have two completely different responses? One of us was enraptured by the story and became emotionally invested, while the other was completely unmoved by the unfolding drama. One of us used up three napkins on tears, while the other asked if I was going to eat all my popcorn. It's like we really *did* see two different movies!

I believe God uses how we view things to move us into His purpose.

Recently, Tom and I were watching the news on television as one world crisis after another was reported. I was multitasking by scrolling through Facebook on my phone, barely paying attention to what was being said. Suddenly, Tom jumped up.

"Did you see that?" He paced the floor, clearly bothered by what he saw.

"Thousands of war refugees need food and water," he said, and immediately headed to the computer to make an online donation before I could even update my Facebook status.

We both observed the story, but only one of us *viewed it* in such a way that led to action. Tom was captivated by the need and was moved by it. He jumped into God's Kingdom purpose and became part of the solution in a small but tangible way.

In today's reading, Habakkuk is clearly burdened. In the first week together, we saw how he begins his prayer with a frustrated cry: "How long, O LORD?" What is he complaining about? What does he see that is worth giving God an earful?

He sees injustice and misery.

He sees destruction and violence.

He sees people who love to argue and fight, and a legal system that has become paralyzed.

He sees wickedness all around him.

His heart is heavy, and it seems like he is the only one who even cares about what's going on.

Habakkuk's burden causes him to do something. It is the reason he writes the book!

You could say that his burden helps lead Habakkuk to his vision, his purpose, and his calling.

I wonder if you can relate to Habakkuk's struggle. Perhaps you are shocked by people's indifference to a particular injustice that you've witnessed. Or you find yourself glued to a certain story on the news, and you can't shake the feeling that you should do something about it. Maybe you're caring for small children or for an elderly parent, and your heart is filled with the burden of seeing to their needs. Perhaps you are surprised by tears that seem to spring out of nowhere when you meet a teen mom who is struggling to provide for her baby.

Or, maybe you just can't stand to see poorly written restaurant menus. God moves in each of us in different ways. Not every burden comes with tears and deep emotion (although poorly written restaurant menus are certainly gut-wrenching). Sometimes it's simply a thought that persists. An idea that won't go away.

Something that seems to sit in the back of your mind, and you just can't shake it.

What burdens you? Could it be that *your* burden will help lead you to discover your purpose and calling? Let's see where this takes us today.

READ

This is the message that the prophet Habakkuk
　　received in a vision.

How long, O LORD, must I call for help?
But you do not listen!
"Violence is everywhere!" I cry,
　　but you do not come to save.
Must I forever see these evil deeds?
　　Why must I watch all this misery?
Wherever I look,
　　I see destruction and violence.
I am surrounded by people
　　who love to argue and fight.
The law has become paralyzed,
　　and there is no justice in the courts.
The wicked far outnumber the righteous,
　　so that justice has become perverted.

HABAKKUK 1:1-4

REFLECT

Notice and highlight the following words: "I cry"; "I forever see"; "I watch"; "I look"; "I am surrounded."

RESPOND

1. How would you finish the following sentences? Be as specific as possible as you fill in the blanks.

I find myself burdened by _____

_____

_____

_____

_____

I always notice when _____

_____

_____

_____

_____

It bothers me to see _____

_____

_____

_____

_____

I can't understand why it doesn't bother other people when __

_____

_____

_____

_____

_____

I empathize with the pain of others because of this pain I've experienced in the past: _____

_____

_____

_____

_____

_____

2. Write down one action—it can be small or large—that you can do *today* in response to one of the burdens above. A phone call, a letter, a gift, a batch of brownies, a care package, a donation . . . don't put it off until tomorrow.

Today, I will _____

_____

_____

_____

_____

_____

_____

.... Day Three ....
WHEN DO YOU EXPERIENCE JOY?

"I will be joyful in the God of my salvation."
HABAKKUK 3:18

I HATE TO BREAK THIS TO YOU, but the prophetic books of the Old Testament aren't brimming with happiness. Although there's really great, important stuff in there, butterflies and rainbows generally don't come shooting out of the pages when you read them.

That's okay, though. These books weren't written to make you feel comfortable. Each is filled with messages of judgment and redemption, destruction and hope, and Habakkuk fits right in there with the rest of them with his writings. His nation, after all, is rife with corruption and all kinds of violence. God tells Habakkuk that He is about to bring in the Babylonians to deliver some wrath, and all hell is about to break loose. No wonder the prophet is a little tense.

But I see something else in these pages.

Something unexpected.

I see joy.

Now, because I like the way Habakkuk 3 fits in today's topics, I'm going to cheat just a little bit and skip to the end of Habakkuk's book to show you this. Bear with me as I give you the lowdown.

After God tells Habakkuk about impending doom, Habakkuk does something strange.

He writes a poetic song.

It's a comforting song that ends with . . . a call to rejoice.

I believe that when faced with grave danger and trouble, Habakkuk turned to his creative gift—his calling as a Temple musician—to offer hope and healing to his nation.

Music, poetry, and praise were woven into the fabric of the Israelites' relationship with God, as a way of expressing thanks, worship, and humility. David, even before he became a king, sang and played an instrument. Psalm means "song," and David wrote many of the ones found in the Bible.

For Habakkuk, these same inspired outlets brought him joy. And in turn, he was able to bring comfort to others. The entire third chapter of his book is a song that he wrote and sang. Here are the final few verses:

> Even though the fig trees have no blossoms,
>   and there are no grapes on the vines;
> even though the olive crop fails,
>   and the fields lie empty and barren;
> even though the flocks die in the fields,
>   and the cattle barns are empty,
> yet I will rejoice in the LORD!
>   I will be joyful in the God of my salvation!
> The Sovereign LORD is my strength!
>   He makes me as surefooted as a deer,
>   able to tread upon the heights.
>
> HABAKKUK 3:17-19

I wonder if Habakkuk ever thought it was silly to learn to write poetry. Or to set words to music. Maybe he wrestled with the dilemma of whether he should only focus on the prophetic side—the solemn side—of his job and leave the creative parts for someone else.

I, for one, am glad he followed his heart. These particular verses have helped me in my own life, some two thousand years later, to remember God's goodness in the face of difficult times. Habakkuk's words still bring comfort and cheer.

God used Habakkuk's creative gift for an eternal purpose.

He is still doing this today.

Like Habakkuk, my joy—creating art through words and paint—became part of my purpose and calling. Now, it took me a long time to find that joy. I was well into my thirties before I ever picked up a paintbrush. I was fifty when I wrote my first book. I was not an early bloomer. But somehow I rediscovered something from my childhood: the pleasure of creating. What started as an outlet for stress became something that God could later use, not just for my own fulfillment, but to help others.

How about you?

Can you think of a time, perhaps from your childhood, when you felt pure joy?

What was it that made you feel happy and fulfilled? Do you still feel that way? Let's spend some time exploring today. We aren't going to jump to any big conclusions or make any grandiose statements. We're simply going to think about the gifts you enjoy and the moments in life that bring you pleasure.

READ

Their trust should be in God, who richly gives us all we need for our enjoyment. 1 TIMOTHY 6:17

Whatever is good and perfect is a gift coming down to us from God our Father, who created all the lights in the heavens. He never changes or casts a shifting shadow. JAMES 1:17

REFLECT

If God has given you good gifts, do you believe He wants to see you enjoy them? Think about the things, the experiences, and the activities that bring you joy. Do you allow yourself time and space to make them part of your life? Can you see this as a way of saying a big thank-you to God?

RESPOND

1. As a child, I loved to _____

_____

_____

_____

2. I feel happy when I _____

_____

_____

_____

3. I feel I am my "best self" when _____

_____

_____

_____

_____

4. People tell me that I'm good at _____

_____

_____

5. When I feel stressed, my favorite de-stressing activity is _____

_____

_____

_____

_____

_____

6. When I see others in distress, I offer help by _____

_____

_____

_____

_____

_____

7. This week, do one activity that simply brings you joy. Write it out here: _____

_____

_____

_____

_____

_____

8. How can you create more space for joy? _____

_____

_____

_____

_____

_____

················ *Day Four* ···············
WHERE ARE YOUR WOUNDS?
···

"In this time of our deep need, help us again."
HABAKKUK 1:5

MY FRIEND MARY DEMUTH is one of the kindest people I know. She cooks for friends, writes books, gardens, and has raised three wonderful children. Her Instagram feed is filled with photos of everyday beauty that she finds: delicious food, family, and walks in the woods. Mary is one of those people who seems to look right into your soul when she talks with you. It's as if you know instantly that anything you say will be safe with her. She is smart and witty, and it's no surprise that people ask her to come and share her story with their group.

But Mary's story begins with deep wounds.

Her childhood should have been a happy one. She should have had two parents who loved her and protected her, and she should have had carefree adventures to fill her days. Instead, she experienced loneliness and neglect. As an only child of a divorced hippie mom and an absent father, she was often left with an uncaring babysitter.

When she was only five, two neighbor boys asked the babysitter if they could take Mary out to play. But they didn't take her to a playground—they took her to the woods and raped her. The sexual abuse continued for a while, and little Mary retreated into a shell to escape the pain. She remembers watching the tree limbs sway overhead as the abuse happened, and wishing she could fly away like a bird into those branches.

Later, as a teenager, she became a Christian and hoped that her newfound faith would magically erase all the pain from her childhood wounds.

It didn't.

Though her wounds did eventually heal, it was not instant, and it was not magic. It took years for Mary to find a place free from the hurts. In her book *The Wall Around Your Heart*, she writes,

> Seeing my past, particularly the relationships there, as a gift has been the linchpin to the greatest healing in my life. I can be like Joseph [a future leader of Israel whose jealous brothers sold him into slavery as a teen and years later were saved by Joseph when famine gripped the land; see Genesis 37–50], who said, "You intended to harm me, but God intended it for good to accomplish what is now being done, the saving of many lives" (Genesis 50:20, NIV).[1]

And there's something else: Mary began sharing her story. As she did so, she allowed her wounds to become a place of healing for others. The tenderness with which she relates to people who are hurting from sexual trauma comes from a place of deep knowing. The hope that she is able to share comes with a richness and resonance that sparks hope and life in those she touches.

Mary's wounded places became a source of purpose in her life. A foundation for hope.

Perhaps your wounds aren't as horrific as those that Mary experienced. But maybe they feel as if they will never heal. Maybe you, like Mary (and like all of us, really), struggle with wondering why this situation was allowed to happen to you. No matter how big or small your wounds may be, you may never have answers that fully satisfy your questions. I would not presume to pull a quick or easy resolution out of my pocket; life is far too complex for that.

I do believe, though, that every place you have been wounded is a place where grace—somehow—can happen.

It is a place where your purpose may begin to take shape.

It makes me think of 2 Corinthians 1:4: "He comforts us in all our troubles so that we can comfort others. When they are troubled, we will be able to give them the same comfort God has given us."

Our wounds bring us deep questions and longings, but they can also create a sense of purpose as we find ourselves giving comfort to others, just as we find comfort in God's healing love.

Where are you wounded? Where are those places that are still tender to the touch? Would you consider allowing God to take those places and use them for something good?

READ

The LORD is my shepherd;
   I have all that I need.
He lets me rest in green meadows;
    he leads me beside peaceful streams.
   He renews my strength.

He guides me along right paths,
　　bringing honor to his name.
Even when I walk
　　through the darkest valley,
I will not be afraid,
　　for you are close beside me.
Your rod and your staff
　　protect and comfort me.
You prepare a feast for me
　　in the presence of my enemies.
You honor me by anointing my head with oil.
　　My cup overflows with blessings.
Surely your goodness and unfailing love will
　　　　pursue me
　　all the days of my life,
and I will live in the house of the LORD
　　forever.

PSALM 23

REFLECT

Meditate on Psalm 23 and these additional verses.

He comforts us in all our troubles so that we can comfort
others. When they are troubled, we will be able to give them
the same comfort God has given us.　2 CORINTHIANS 1:4

He heals the brokenhearted
　　and binds up their wounds.
PSALM 147:3, NIV

In his kindness God called you to share in his eternal glory
by means of Christ Jesus. So after you have suffered a little

while, he will restore, support, and strengthen you, and he will place you on a firm foundation.   I PETER 5:10

RESPOND

1. Where are your wounded places? Are you able to write them down? _____

    _____

    _____

    _____

    _____

2. How have your wounds affected your relationships with others? With God? _____

    _____

    _____

    _____

    _____

3. What strengths do you have as a result of your wounds? ____

    _____

    _____

    _____

    _____

    _____

4. Do you relate to others who have been wounded in the same ways you have? _____

    _____

    _____

    _____

    _____

5. Can you think of some ways that your wounds can be used as a starting point for others' healing? _____

_____

_____

_____

_____

_____

_____

Day Five
WHY NOT?

"I am doing something in your own day, something you wouldn't believe."

HABAKKUK 1:5

SEVERAL YEARS AGO, a stray donkey showed up on our driveway. Yes, a *donkey*. After a ridiculous rescue scene (and by rescue, I mean Tom pushing, pulling, bribing, cajoling, and otherwise forcing the donkey into our pasture), we tried to find his owners. Nobody claimed him. We felt sorry for the abandoned animal, plus we sort of fell in love with the guy, and so we ended up keeping him. He wasn't much to look at. His short, stubby legs were scratched, and his head and neck had deep gashes from barbed wire. Though scared and timid at first, he eventually warmed to our attention and became a member of the family. We named him Flash.

Flash spent his days hanging out with some fat cows who lived just over the fence, chewing their cuds and watching the world go by. One afternoon, a neighbor's three thoroughbred horses got loose and wound up on our property. While we waited for their owner to arrive, we put them into the pasture with Flash. The gorgeous stallions danced and pranced in the golden sunset. At first Flash didn't notice them, but then he opened his eyes wide and shook his head as if to get the cobwebs out.

"This oughta be interesting!" I said as we watched the scene unfold. Flash suddenly had a choice to make: he could stay with the cows, who were familiar but unexciting, or he could join the band of thoroughbreds, who looked as if they were the stars of a horse ballet. Flash, with his short legs, long ears, shaggy coat, and oversized head, was completely outclassed by these horses, with their long legs, graceful necks, and flowing manes. He hesitated for just a moment and then ran over to join them.

What a sight! My dusty little donkey with the three stunning horses! He circled, spun, bucked, and danced with them. It was as if Flash said to himself, "Why not?" and decided to leave the company of the safe cows for the adventure of running with horses.

That day, Flash discovered greatness within him. He found that there was more to life than just watching it pass by. He took a chance, and it changed him forever.

Maybe that's a simple story, but it struck me so deeply at the time that I made profound changes in my own life. It inspired me to stop wishing for my big chance and to go out and actually take one. So often, we find ourselves stuck in situations like Flash did: perfectly safe, just fine, so easy. We see others out there doing something great, and we wish we could get out there too. We think how wonderful it must be to be born with such talent, to be given opportunities, to be able to do big things. *If only I'd been so lucky*, we say.

But here's the thing:

Each day we are given opportunities to do great things.

No matter how small or seemingly insignificant those things are, we can do them with excellence. Why not? And each day we are given the chance to be the best we can be. Why not? We can step out and find something new, something that we feel outclassed and outshone in, and simply do it anyway. Why not?

You see, I've found that asking why is counterproductive. I can think of a million reasons why I will fail. There are a bazillion ways my ideas lack merit. But when I rephrase it as "Why not?" it shines a whole new light on things.

"Why not?" sounds like possibility knocking. It sounds like taking a deep breath and plunging in. It sounds like a pencil on paper as you figure out ways to make something happen. It sounds like a jet engine taking flight for an adventure.

"Why not?" unlocks the door to purpose.

READ

As word spread about Jesus' healing miracles, large crowds began to seek Him out. When more than five thousand men, women, and children gathered, Jesus fed them all from five loaves and two fish that His disciples brought to Him.

> Immediately after this, Jesus insisted that his disciples get back into the boat and cross to the other side of the lake, while he sent the people home. After sending them home, he went up into the hills by himself to pray. Night fell while he was there alone.
>
> Meanwhile, the disciples were in trouble far away from land, for a strong wind had risen, and they were fighting heavy waves. About three o'clock in the morning Jesus came toward them, walking on the water. When the disciples saw him walking on the water, they were terrified. In their fear, they cried out, "It's a ghost!"

But Jesus spoke to them at once. "Don't be afraid," he said. "Take courage. I am here!"

Then Peter called to him, "Lord, if it's really you, tell me to come to you, walking on the water."

"Yes, come," Jesus said.

So Peter went over the side of the boat and walked on the water toward Jesus. But when he saw the strong wind and the waves, he was terrified and began to sink. "Save me, Lord!" he shouted.

Jesus immediately reached out and grabbed him. "You have so little faith," Jesus said. "Why did you doubt me?"

When they climbed back into the boat, the wind stopped. Then the disciples worshiped him. "You really are the Son of God!" they exclaimed.   MATTHEW 14:22-33

REFLECT

Put yourself in the disciples' boat. Would you be one of the disciples saying, "Peter, why are you doing that?" or would you be like Peter and say, "Why not?"

RESPOND

1. What did Peter have to overcome in order to put his feet over the side of the boat? _____

    _____

    _____

2. How did he stay on top of the water? What can you learn from this? _____

    _____

    _____

    _____

3. Are you stuck on the "why" questions? How would asking "Why not?" change your thinking? _____

_____

_____

_____

_____

4. List five things you wish you could do, or things you'd like to do. Maybe they are already on your bucket list, or maybe they are directly related to your purpose.

1. _____

_____

2. _____

_____

3. _____

_____

4. _____

_____

5. _____

_____

5. Now ask yourself: Why not? What's keeping you from taking steps to accomplish them? _____

_____

_____

_____

_____

_____

Week Three
POSITIONED TO SEE CLEARLY

· ·

"Begin, be bold, and venture to be wise."

HORACE

IN WEEK ONE, we saw how our friend Habakkuk looked at his circumstances and got honest with God. Honesty is the best and wisest foundation to build upon because it leads us to think about God's purpose *in* us: for us to be loved, to belong, and to grow.

In week two, we turned a corner and looked at ways God uses our questions to help guide us. We asked the five W questions: who, what, where, when, and why. It was a lot to think about and process, and I'll admit I'm still working through some of those questions myself. I encourage you to feel free to revisit these activities throughout the rest of our study.

This week, we'll continue to look at practical ways to activate God's other purposes—ones that are uniquely suited for your dreams and passions. Keep your paintbrush handy (and your pencil sharp) as we fill in more blank spaces in our underpainting.

Let's jump to chapter 2 of Habakkuk for our inspiration. Right off the bat, our prophet does something we can make note of.

He puts himself in the right position to hear from God.

He climbs up to his watchtower (verse 1).

Habakkuk is serious about getting direction. Whether literally or figuratively speaking, going to the watchtower shows us that his head is in the game. He's done talking; he's finished complaining. Now he wants a vision. And so he climbs. It is right here that we will perch, alongside Habakkuk, for the rest of this week.

Day One
VIEW FROM ABOVE

"I will climb up to my watchtower."
HABAKKUK 2:1

YEARS AGO, I took piano lessons at a local college. I'd always loved to play the piano by ear, but I wanted to be able to read music, too, so I could play from sheet music and hymnals. The lessons went well, until the day my teacher informed me that there would be a recital at the end of the semester.

"Oh, no," I responded. "I'm not interested in participating in a recital. I'm simply learning to play the piano for my own enjoyment."

My teacher looked at me with a blank stare, as if I'd just said something in a foreign language. After a moment she spoke slowly, as if she were explaining something to a child.

"Rachel. The piano is a performance instrument. It is *made* to be played in a group, or with other instruments, or as an accompaniment to singers. *It is for the enjoyment of others.* This is why we have recitals . . . so you can become excellent for the benefit of your listeners."

She shuffled the music in front of us and muttered, "Taking piano lessons for your own benefit is like taking voice lessons so you can sound better in the shower. It's just ludicrous."

Ouch.

Her point was well taken. When it came to understanding the purpose of the piano, I had the wrong mind-set. I thought that getting better at something I enjoyed was simply to bring *me* more joy. And while it certainly did do that, I learned that my focus had been much too small.

The same is true when we approach our life purpose. You see, when we approach it from the perspective of fulfilling *our own personal enjoyment*, we are missing the greater picture.

What we need is a bigger perspective. Our life purpose is tied to what God is doing in the greater world around us.

God wants to take what we have and use it to affect others in a positive way.

Habakkuk changes his perspective as he waits for God's answer and direction. You could say he gets a bigger picture. From high above, he can see for miles. His vantage point has changed, and he can view his surroundings from a new perspective—an eternal one. From his watchtower, Habakkuk can turn and see 360 degrees, all the way to the horizon, not just to the four walls of his Temple home.

His circle has widened.

In the same way, we need to metaphorically climb up a spiritual watchtower for another view of things. God's purpose for your life is much bigger than figuring out what you're good at and then just doing that for the remainder of your days. It's bigger than finding something you enjoy or simply solving problems.

God's purpose for you will always be about the wider circle—the people around you in your sphere. It will stretch in all directions, creating a 360-degree panorama as far as you can see.

God's purpose for you extends *beyond* you.

READ

I will climb up to my watchtower
    and stand at my guardpost.
There I will wait to see what the LORD says
    and how he will answer my complaint.

HABAKKUK 2:1

Forgetting the past and looking forward to what lies
ahead, I press on to reach the end of the race and receive
the heavenly prize for which God, through Christ Jesus,
is calling us.   PHILIPPIANS 3:13-14

REFLECT

It took an effort for Habakkuk to reach a new perspective and mindset. It may have been daunting to face flight after flight of stairs, or perhaps a series of rickety ladders, to take him to the top of a watchtower for a different view.

Are you willing to put effort into seeking God for His view of your life purpose?

Is the perspective you have now too small? Is it "me" centered or "others" centered?

RESPOND

1. What is one dream or desire of yours that has perhaps been too small?_____

   _____

   _____

   _____

   _____

2. How might gaining a greater view change the way you see that dream?_____

   _____

   _____

   _____

   _____

3. Fill in the blanks to help you envision your dream.

   I want to become _____

   _____ so that _____

   _____

   _____

   _____

4. List three people in your circle of relationships who are currently affected in a positive way by your life. How might this *already* fit in with God's greater purposes?

   1. _____

      _____

   2. _____

      _____

   3. _____

      _____

.... *Day Two* ....
WATCH FOR ENEMIES

. . . .

"Will they succeed forever in their heartless conquests?"

HABAKKUK 1:17

"I'LL BE WEARING a white ball cap when I get off the plane," Tom told me on the phone. "That should make it easier to spot me in the crowd."

White ball cap. White ball cap. I scanned the throngs of people streaming through the security door and into the baggage claim area.

Goodness! Why are so many people wearing white ball caps today? It was like a sea of white ball caps, a tidal wave of matching hats coming toward me.

I stood on tiptoe and craned my neck to try to see around a large person who had inconveniently planted himself in front of me. Now this person was waving his arms.

Oh, for crying out loud. Really? Can't see a thing around your carcass.

I pictured my husband's face, imagined his height, and thought of the black jacket he'd have on. Surely he'd gotten off the plane by now. *If only I could see . . .*

Then the person in front of me spoke. "Rachel! Hellooo! It's me."

Yep, you guessed it. It was my husband. In a white ball cap, of course. Waving his arms and trying to get my attention.

Good thing he is aware of my problem. It's a real thing, and I'm sure there is a name for it, but I can't recognize familiar faces in large crowds of people. I just sort of panic, things go kind of fuzzy on me, and I can't for the life of me find the person I'm looking for. It's awful. Apparently even clothing hints don't help.

And speaking of not helping—my family teases me about it to no end.

Oh, it's a funny story all right. Go ahead and laugh; I don't mind. Because it reminds me of another problem: how difficult it can be to recognize negative thought patterns and habits, even when we are looking directly at them.

Sometimes the biggest obstacle to discovering our life purpose is . . . well, ourselves.

Negative thoughts, insecurities, self-talk, fear—somewhere along the way we've developed habits that keep us from stepping out into being all that we can be. The trouble is, we don't realize these things are right in front of us, even when they're wearing white ball caps and waving their little arms and jumping up and down.

Climb the rickety ladder with me, back up to our watchtower from yesterday's verse in Habakkuk: "I will climb up to my watchtower." High upon the city wall in Jerusalem sits a tiny room with windows on every side. It houses a watchman. This person's job is to be on the lookout for enemy warriors and to sound an alarm as soon as they appear on the horizon. The farther away the enemy is, the more time the watchman can give the people below to organize themselves, grab their weapons, and be prepared to fight.

The watchman is trained to know what to look for. Groups of marauders on horseback with gleaming weapons would be a good clue. But for us, it's not always so simple. We need some help to recognize the enemies that hold us back. Sometimes we've made friends with the very things that are seeking to destroy us.

Fear of Failure, anyone? He's an old pal of mine—we go way back. Perhaps you know him too. He's the one who consistently reminds you of every mistake and misstep you've ever made. He wouldn't want you to embarrass yourself or come up short in any way, so he tells you that it's better not to try.

Comparison? This guy points out all the people who seem superior to you—who have more talent, are more connected, and have better hair. With his lies, he convinces you that you'll always be the also-ran in the race.

How about our buddy Not Enough? This enemy lurks around in the shadows, forever whispering insults that thwart your ability to move forward.

Oh, we could go on and on. Perfectionism, Doubt, Insecurity, Lack of Confidence, Anxiety, and even Laziness . . . they all mount their attacks to make sure you don't live your fullest life. They don't want you to discover and fulfill your God-given purpose.

The first step to victory is to recognize your enemies before they get close enough to do damage. Then you can fight strategically and effectively to become all you can be.

READ

When you go out to fight your enemies and you face horses
and chariots and an army greater than your own, do not be
afraid. The LORD your God, who brought you out of the land

of Egypt, is with you! When you prepare for battle, the priest must come forward to speak to the troops. He will say to them, "Listen to me, all you men of Israel! Do not be afraid as you go out to fight your enemies today! Do not lose heart or panic or tremble before them. For the LORD your God is going with you! He will fight for you against your enemies, and he will give you victory!"   DEUTERONOMY 20:1-4

I love you, LORD;
    you are my strength.
The LORD is my rock, my fortress, and my savior;
    my God is my rock, in whom I find protection.
He is my shield, the power that saves me,
    and my place of safety.
I called on the LORD, who is worthy of praise,
    and he saved me from my enemies.

PSALM 18:1-3

REFLECT

What are your enemies' names?

- Fear
- Anxiety
- Perfectionism
- Comparison
- Complacency
- Inferiority
- Impatience
- Blame
- Inability to Trust (God or others)

The Bible tells us that for people who follow Jesus, none of these things have power or control over us. We can walk in freedom from them through the power of God's presence. The more of our lives we give to Him, the less we have to worry about these enemies wreaking havoc.

RESPOND

1. How have these enemies kept you from stepping into a more purposeful life? _____

    _____

    _____

    _____

    _____

2. What might your life look like when they no longer play a role?

    _____

    _____

    _____

    _____

3. Commit to following God's truth today, and begin by writing it out: _____ does not have power over me any longer. I choose (the opposite) _____ each day, by the grace and power of God.

4. This week, do one thing that fights your enemy. Sign up for a class, volunteer for a solo part, start a painting, make a phone call you've been afraid to make. I think you know what it is.

5. Do one other thing—the thing you think you can't do— without expecting perfection.

6. Memorize Romans 8:37:

    Overwhelming victory is ours through Christ, who loved us.

Day Three
FIND THE RIGHT BATTLES TO FIGHT

"You went out to rescue your chosen people."

HABAKKUK 3:13

ON A TRIP TO COLORADO several years ago, our family camped near the base of Mount Elbert. My husband, who would have been a professional mountain climber had I not come along and spoiled his plans, decided to take a day hike up the famous fourteener (a peak that is over 14,000 feet in elevation) while the rest of us lounged near the campfire.

He set off early, eager to reach the summit before afternoon storms could roll in. As Tom would later recount, the climb was arduous but went well, as Mount Elbert is one of the easier Rockies to conquer. By the time he reached the top, Tom had depleted all his water and granola bars, but he was exhilarated with his success! He pulled out his camera to capture the moment.

But as he looked north he realized, with horrible dismay, that he'd climbed the *wrong mountain*. Mount Elbert stood dauntingly aloof beyond the next ridge . . . and the next ridge . . . and the next ridge . . .

Not to be beaten, my mountaineer guy managed to climb not one but several mountains that day, eventually reaching Mount Elbert's summit without another drop of water or bite to eat. When he returned many hours later, utterly exhausted, I think his exact words were "I never want to do that again."

There's nothing worse than finding you've climbed the wrong mountain or fought the wrong battle. It's not only a sad waste of energy but a waste of talent and focus that could have been used far more productively and effectively. You may eventually make it to the right place, but you may be so weary that you can't enjoy it.

This brings us back to Habakkuk in the watchtower. This week we're thinking about how the right vantage point is important for discovering our purpose. And what could be more important than being on the lookout for the *right* battles to fight? The watchman has a clear view of which areas need immediate attention, where reinforcements are needed, and how to best use the available resources.

Assuming the right position means we are able to see the right places to put our energy and talents.

You know, I've often made the mistake of thinking that because I'm so busy, I *must* be making progress in my life purpose. Unfortunately, busy does not always mean purposeful or productive, or even healthy. Sometimes, busy just means busy. It's good to take a hard look at the things that fill our lives and learn to be intentional about how we spend our time and energy. Rather than fighting every battle, or saying yes to every activity that comes our way, we should commit to choosing (as best we can) those things that are positive, productive, and purposeful.

Please note that "positive, productive, and purposeful" does not mean that there isn't time for rest and relaxation, two things that are vital to our health and well-being. My point here is that we should make wise decisions: Should we spend an extra hour on Facebook each night, or get an extra hour of sleep? Should we sign up for another weeknight activity, when we are out every evening already? Sometimes we feel victimized by our schedule when, in reality, we have control over most things on it.

Discovering, preparing for, and developing our sense of purpose takes time and thoughtfulness. It takes attentiveness and consideration. When all your time is taken up with busyness, there is nothing left over for purposeful growth.

Today, let's use our "watchtower positioning" to be on the lookout for time wasters, energy drainers, and purpose saboteurs.

READ

As Jesus and the disciples continued on their way to Jerusalem, they came to a certain village where a woman named Martha welcomed him into her home. Her sister, Mary, sat at the Lord's feet, listening to what he taught. But Martha was distracted by the big dinner she was preparing. She came to Jesus and said, "Lord, doesn't it seem unfair to you that my sister just sits here while I do all the work? Tell her to come and help me."

But the Lord said to her, "My dear Martha, you are worried and upset over all these details! There is only one thing worth being concerned about. Mary has discovered it, and it will not be taken away from her." LUKE 10:38-42

Teach us to realize the brevity of life,
so that we may grow in wisdom.

PSALM 90:12

REFLECT

Are you busy—without being purposeful? In Luke's story of Martha and Mary recounted on the previous page, do you identify with Martha, the sister who is distracted by all the things that must be done? Write down on the following lines the things that distract you from the important things in life. _____

_____

_____

_____

_____

_____

_____

_____

_____

Do you feel that you are intentional with your time and energy? Reflect on your "wrong battles." What would be the "right battles" to put your time, energy, and talents toward? _____

_____

_____

_____

_____

_____

_____

_____

RESPOND

1. Take a few moments to assess how your time (your currency for resources and energy) is spent. What does a typical day or week look like? _____

   _____

   _____

   _____

   _____

   _____

   _____

2. When do you have time to rest and recharge? When do prayer and Bible reading fit in? _____

   _____

   _____

   _____

   _____

   _____

3. Is every moment spoken for? Are there activities you can eliminate? _____

   _____

   _____

   _____

   _____

Do you have time to learn something new or develop your skills and talents? Sometimes simply observing where your time goes helps you know which battles to fight. On the following chart, pencil in your time commitments to see where your time is spent.

WHERE DOES MY TIME GO?

Time	Monday	Tuesday	Wednesday	Thursday	Friday	Saturday	Sunday
6:00							
7:00							
8:00							
9:00							
10:00							
11:00							
12:00							
1:00							
2:00							
3:00							
4:00							
5:00							
6:00							
7:00							
8:00							
9:00							

Day Four
NOTICE CLUES

"I will wait to see what the LORD says and how he will answer."

HABAKKUK 2:1

"AHA! Colonel Mustard, in the lounge, with a knife!"

One of my favorite childhood board games was *Clue*. Remember that game? It was a perfect rainy afternoon pastime as my brother and sister and I would move our pieces around the board, along with a collection of tiny weapons. I always tried to be Miss Scarlet, clearly the most glamorous of the suspects, and thereby the least likely person to have committed the crime. (At least, that's how my reasoning went at the time.)

The whole point of the game was to collect evidence about a murder that had taken place in a mansion by following the clues given by other players. Using the power of deduction and the process of elimination, it was a race to see who could make the triumphant accusation and win the game. It seemed that my brother was always a step ahead of me and could solve the mystery long before I could.

Like Clue, discerning your life purpose can feel like a detective story.

We move through life, collecting bits of information and evidence that put us on a trail of discovery. Sometimes we make a guess and shout, "Professor Plum, in the library, with a candlestick!" only to find that we've misconstrued the clues along the way. Fortunately, rather than being a win-lose pursuit like a board game, life gives us plenty of chances to keep on playing. In fact, discovering our purpose may be just the beginning of a whole new game.

In Habakkuk 2, the prophet has climbed up into the watchtower, and like him, we must keep our eyes peeled for indications, evidence, and movements. We are tuned in to what's ordinary, what's normal, and what's expected, as well as to new developments, interests, and changes. A careful observer takes it all in, weighs the information, and considers the clues. Opening our eyes and utilizing our senses can help us draw conclusions about our own strengths and abilities.

Let's have a little fun today, shall we? You can be the glamorous Miss Scarlet, and I'll be Mrs. Peacock. Only instead of solving a crime, we are simply looking for clues.

READ

I want them to be encouraged and knit together by strong ties of love. I want them to have complete confidence that they understand God's mysterious plan, which is Christ himself. In him lie hidden all the treasures of wisdom and knowledge. COLOSSIANS 2:2-3

When I first came to you, dear brothers and sisters, I didn't use lofty words and impressive wisdom to tell you God's secret plan [mystery]. For I decided that while I was with you I would forget everything except Jesus Christ, the one who was crucified. I came to you in weakness—timid and trembling. And my message and my preaching were very plain. Rather than using clever and persuasive speeches, I relied only on the power of the Holy Spirit. I did this so you would trust not in human wisdom but in the power of God.

Yet when I am among mature believers, I do speak with words of wisdom, but not the kind of wisdom that belongs to this world or to the rulers of this world, who are soon forgotten. No, the wisdom we speak of is the mystery of God—his plan that was previously hidden, even though he made it for our ultimate glory before the world began.

1 CORINTHIANS 2:1-7

It is impossible to please God without faith. Anyone who wants to come to him must believe that God exists and that he rewards those who sincerely seek him.   HEBREWS 11:6

REFLECT

It seems God is a good mystery writer because there are times when everything is not always crystal clear to us. But according to the above verse from Hebrews, He rewards those who seek Him. He reveals His will and plan to those who are actively looking.

Can you view the "hiding" of His purposes not as an inconvenient obstacle but as a beautiful way in which He unfolds His will and plan?

RESPOND

1. Write down an experience in the past that did not make sense to you at the time, but you now have some perspective about:

_____

_____

_____

_____

_____

2. Are there certain negative or positive themes that seem to show up repeatedly in the experiences of your life? _____

_____

_____

_____

_____

_____

3. If you could change one thing about your life right now, what would it be?_____

_____

_____

_____

_____

_____

4. Describe the things that are "normal and usual" to you that others find "different and unusual." (Example: you love roughing it in the outdoors, while others consider a hotel stay to be "roughing it.") _____

_____

_____

_____

_____

_____

_____

5. If money was not an issue, what is something you would want to do every day as a job?_____

_____

_____

_____

_____

_____

_____

6. Are there ways you can indulge this passion in some capacity?

_____

_____

_____

_____

_____

_____

7. What is something a detective might uncover about your personality that you keep hidden from sight?_____

_____

_____

_____

_____

8. Read Psalm 139 and then answer this question: How does knowing that God has uniquely created you affect how you see Him and His "mysterious" ways?_____

_____

_____

_____

_____

Day Five
SEE YOUR GIFTS

"The Sovereign LORD is my strength."
HABAKKUK 3:19

ONE OF MY FRIENDS is an amazing gift giver. She remembers special occasions like birthdays and anniversaries, and she celebrates my life's big events with thoughtful gestures. For example, to honor the birth of my first grandchild, my friend gave me a beautiful silver necklace with an engraved charm. And with each new grandchild who has come, another little box containing a new initialed charm has arrived in the mail. She knows how much I love those babies, and she has found a way to express her love in a way that's meaningful to me. Every time I fasten the clasp of my necklace, I feel loved.

Gifts say as much about the giver as they do about the recipient. The time and care that go into choosing just the right gift show the giver's thoughtfulness, generosity, and love. There is a whole group of special gifts called *spiritual gifts* that God gives to us. They are often different from the natural talents and abilities we immediately think of when we look for our purpose. Spiritual gifts are given specifically to God's people—those who follow Jesus—to help prepare them for service to Him and to use for the common good.

Spiritual gifts reveal God's care for His people and reflect His design for each individual's life.

When these are operating in your life, you'll often find that you're tapped into great joy as you use them. There is a connection to God that gives you a sense of purpose and satisfaction.

Spiritual gifts are mentioned in 1 Corinthians 12; Romans 12; and 1 Peter 4. Here is a list:

Prophecy (speaking forth God's truth)

Serving

Teaching

Encouraging

Giving

Leadership

Mercy

Words of wisdom

Words of knowledge

Faith

Healing

Miracles

Discernment

Tongues (speaking in an unknown language during prayer and religious worship)

Interpretation of tongues

Helps

Prayer

How can you discover your gifts? Often, your spiritual gifts are revealed by how you respond to situations. Imagine yourself in the watchtower for a moment. From your bird's-eye view, you can see the whole city and surrounding countryside. You see a group of people approaching the city gate, coming to the market. One of the men accidentally steps into a pothole and falls to the ground in pain. There is a flurry of commotion as everyone in the group springs into action. A person with the gift of mercy immediately begins to fashion a splint. Another, with the gift of prayer, asks God for help and healing. The person with the gift of leadership organizes a team to carry the injured man to the hospital. Those with the gift of helps jump in wherever they are needed, some making a stretcher and others assisting the splint maker. One guy shouts, "You guys are doing great!" to the group. His gift of encouragement energizes the others. Another young man with the gift of service notices that the victim is thirsty and fetches some cold water. A lady in the group, a giver, opens her wallet and offers to pay for the medical expenses. And the fellow with the gift of administration starts the paperwork on the whole incident so that everything is properly recorded.

Did you see how each person jumped into a certain role or task? Each one responded with his or her spiritual gift, without even realizing it. The work got done with everyone doing their parts—working together as a beautiful team. One individual could not have done everything alone.

Spiritual gifts are often the underlying motivators for action and for service. Because they are specifically given by God, their operation in your life brings a unique connection to His power and love and to others. It's the spark that allows "service" to become "ministry," which is an exciting part of the Christian life. Your own spiritual gifts are worth seeking out and developing to their fullest as you grow in faith.

READ

In his grace, God has given us different gifts for doing certain things well. So if God has given you the ability to prophesy, speak out with as much faith as God has given you. If your gift is serving others, serve them well. If you are a teacher, teach well. If your gift is to encourage others, be encouraging. If it is giving, give generously. If God has given you leadership ability, take the responsibility seriously. And if you have a gift for showing kindness to others, do it gladly. ROMANS 12:6-8

There are different kinds of spiritual gifts, but the same Spirit is the source of them all. There are different kinds of service, but we serve the same Lord. God works in different ways, but it is the same God who does the work in all of us.

A spiritual gift is given to each of us so we can help each other. To one person the Spirit gives the ability to give wise advice; to another the same Spirit gives a message of special knowledge. The same Spirit gives great faith to another, and to someone else the one Spirit gives the gift of healing. He gives one person the power to perform miracles, and another the ability to prophesy. He gives someone else the ability to discern whether a message is from the Spirit of God or from another spirit. Still another person is given the ability to speak in unknown languages, while another is given the ability to interpret what is being said. It is the one and only Spirit who distributes all these gifts. He alone decides which gift each person should have.   I CORINTHIANS 12:4-11

All of you together are Christ's body, and each of you is a part of it. Here are some of the parts God has appointed for the church: first are apostles, second are prophets, third are teachers, then those who do miracles, those who have the gift of healing, those who can help others, those who have the gift of leadership, those who speak in unknown languages.
I CORINTHIANS 12:27-28

REFLECT

Do you know what spiritual gift(s) you have? Do you feel that any gifts are a part of your life right now? Reflect on the activities that bring you the most satisfaction. Do they fit into any of the spiritual gifts?

RESPOND

1. Read over the list of spiritual gifts. In the scenario about the injured man described in today's reading, how would you have responded? _____

   _____

   _____

   _____

   _____

   _____

2. In what ways do you love helping people? How do you commonly help others? _____

   _____

   _____

   _____

   _____

   _____

   _____

3. What do others thank you for doing? _____

   _____

   _____

   _____

   _____

   _____

4. If you aren't sure what your spiritual gifts are, there are some things you can do to help you discover them.

- Take an assessment test. Some online tests offer simple guidelines.
- Try volunteering in different areas of service. See what things fit well with you!
- Pray. Ask God to reveal your spiritual gifts to you.
- Ask others what gifts they see in you. Often other people can observe things we can't see in ourselves.

Here are a few suggested books about finding God's purpose for your life.

All the Places to Go . . . How Will You Know?, John Ortberg
Embracing Your Second Calling, Dale Hanson Bourke
Fresh Air, Chris Hodges
Own Your Life, Sally Clarkson
Your Best Destiny, Wintley Phipps

Week Four
POISED FOR SUCCESS

. . . .

*"We have only one brief lifetime to prove our faith
and our love for Christ."*

JONI EARECKSON TADA

LAST WEEK WE SAW HABAKKUK climb to his watchtower to get a bigger view of the landscape. He has voiced his honest questions to God and ascended a series of steps and ladders, and now he's settling in to wait for an answer. Unfortunately for him, the guard post's small chamber isn't made for comfort. There's no easy chair to sit in, no stack of books to read, no slippers to warm his feet. There's no table to hold a plate of food in case he gets hungry.

There is just enough room to stand.

So standing is just what he does.

Standing is the posture of readiness.

Standing is the physical stance of an alert mental state.

Shoulders square, chin up, poised for action.

Week four of our journey to find purpose is a perfect place to talk about mental postures. Why? Because most of us are natural slouchers. We hit the middle part of most any endeavor and our shoulders start to droop, our heads hang low, and deep sighs of exhaustion escape our lips. To be honest, if it's midafternoon, I'm looking for a corner where I can curl up and take a nap.

The middle is the danger zone.

The middle is where we get bogged down.

The middle is where most of us fail.

It's when the excitement of a shiny beginning has worn off, and the reality of the work involved gets heavy. We begin to question our decisions, look askance at our ideas, and doubt our ability to pull off anything worthwhile.

The middle is where we can't see any results from all our effort.

It's where settling for the status quo seems like a really good option.

Again, we will take a cue from Habakkuk. He is poised for victory, and he is determined to see this vision through. This week, we'll look closely at his five postures for success.

Day One
STAND IN PERSISTENCE

"I will . . . stand at my guardpost."

HABAKKUK 2:1

HABAKKUK IS THE PICTURE of mental alertness. He is all in. He knows it may be a while before he hears from God, but he's got his feet planted and he's not going to rest until he hears something.

Our first guard tower posture is the stance of persistence.

The Google Dictionary defines *persistence* as "firm or obstinate continuance in a course of action in spite of difficulty or opposition." Quite simply, it is most often the difference between failure and success. It's the stick-to-itiveness that keeps a person going no matter what.

The pages of history are filled with characters who faced seemingly insurmountable odds, difficult setbacks, and dramatic failures. Abraham Lincoln, one of my favorite people to study, should have given up at almost every point in his life. Here are some of his highlights—or lowlights—compiled by Matthew Kelly in his book *The Rhythm of Life*:

In 1816 [when Lincoln was seven], Lincoln's family was forced out of their home, and he had to go to work to support them.

In 1818, his mother died.

In 1831, he failed in business.

In 1832, he ran for the Illinois House of Representatives and lost.

In 1832, he lost his job. Later that same year, he decided he wanted to go to law school, but his application was rejected.

In 1833, Lincoln borrowed some money from a friend to begin a business, but by the end of the year he was bankrupt. He spent the next seventeen years paying off that debt.

In 1834, he ran for state legislature again and lost.

In 1835, Lincoln was engaged to be married, but his fiancée died and it broke his heart. In 1836, Lincoln suffered a total nervous breakdown and was confined to his bed for six months.

In 1838, he sought to become Speaker of the state legislature and was defeated.

In 1840, he sought to become elector and was defeated.

In 1843, he ran for Congress and lost.

In 1846, he ran for Congress again; this time he won and finally made his way to Washington.

In 1848, Lincoln ran for reelection to Congress and lost.

In 1849, he sought the job of land officer but was rejected.

In 1854, he ran for Senate of the United States and lost.

In 1856, he sought the vice presidential nomination at his party's national convention. He got fewer than one hundred votes and lost.

In 1858, he ran for the United States Senate again and lost again.

Then, in 1860, Lincoln decided to run for president. . . .

I mean, based on what?

His track record?

He won and went on to become one of the greatest presidents in the history of the United States and one of the finest models of leadership in modern times. In a speech, Lincoln said, "The path was worn and slippery. My foot slipped from under me, knocking the other out of the way, but I recovered and said to myself, 'It's a slip and not a fall.'"[2]

Abraham Lincoln kept standing.

Failure, discouragement, and defeat *will happen* on the journey toward fulfilling your destiny. But the stance of persistence says that no failure is ever final, no discouragement is too great, and no defeat is the end of the story. Instead, it recognizes that these experiences are part of the process to refine our character and clarify our vision. They will help propel us forward into our purpose, if we let them.

No matter how many times you get knocked down, simply get back up into the standing position.

Are you facing the discouragement of the "middle," or feeling the sting of failure? Do you find that your *physical posture* reflects your inner feelings of defeat? I've found that discouragement does make its way into my physical body, and I need this reminder.

Stand up, square your shoulders, and put your chin up. Take a deep breath. Imagine that the determination to persevere is being poured into you. You have all the strength you need to press on. What does that feel like?

Now, imagine that your next steps will be the ones that will put you back on track. Remember, the middle is not the end . . . so keep on standing, my friend.

READ

When troubles of any kind come your way, consider it an opportunity for great joy. For you know that when your faith is tested, your endurance has a chance to grow. So let it grow, for when your endurance is fully developed, you will be perfect and complete, needing nothing.   JAMES 1:2-4

Let us not become weary in doing good, for at the proper time we will reap a harvest if we do not give up.
GALATIANS 6:9, NIV

We also pray that you will be strengthened with all his glorious power so you will have all the endurance and patience you need. May you be filled with joy.
COLOSSIANS 1:11

REFLECT

Nearly every person who has made history—athlete, political figure, activist, writer, and artist—has a story that shows grit and determination. Thomas Edison reportedly said, "Many of life's failures are people who did not realize how close they were to success when they gave up."

All you need to do is stand up one time more than you get knocked down. Your purpose in life will elude you if you lack the determination to keep pursuing it. That's why we are here together, and that's why you will keep getting back up!

RESPOND

1. Make a list of people you admire. What kinds of obstacles have they faced? What kept them going?_____

_____

_____

_____

_____

_____

2. What struggles have you faced in life that required persever-ance? How has past perseverance helped prepare you for your current situation? _____

_____

_____

_____

_____

_____

3. Now that you're in the stance of persistence, what will your next steps be—through the middle, toward your goal? _____

_____

_____

_____

_____

_____

4. Write a completion date for your next steps here: _____

_____

_____

_____

.... *Day Two* ....
FACE YOUR FEARS

. . . .

"My lips quivered with fear."

HABAKKUK 3:16

"I'VE GOT A SPOT on the agenda for you to speak to the board of contractors about the design you're working on for the restaurant space." My colleague's voice on the phone sounded excited about the upcoming meeting.

But she might as well have said, "Here, stand on top of this really high cliff and jump off it with a teeny tiny parachute." Because that's pretty much what I heard. She could not have struck more fear into me if she'd pushed me off that cliff herself. I was terrified of speaking to a group . . . out loud . . . in person.

Just the thought of standing up in front of, say, two people (let alone a whole conference room full of strangers) made my palms sweat. Already I felt myself blacking out. My mouth went dry. I knew I would have to try to get out of it.

"Sounds great! Can't wait!" I heard myself say in response. My mouth was clearly operating on its own just then. I hung up the phone and immediately tried to think up excuses for skipping out on the meeting. If I planned it right, I could be out of the country and off the grid for an extended period of time. Then someone else might cover for me.

Fear of public speaking had a grip on me. It held me hostage, keeping me from any possibility of making presentations or speeches. It made me shift responsibilities to others and take projects I didn't enjoy just so I would not be called upon to speak. It made me find ways to be less than excellent, because nobody ever gets asked to share mediocre ideas.

Fear kept me from reaching my potential and accomplishing my secret dream of helping others in a bigger arena. It prevented me from stepping into my purpose.

I realized in that moment, with the phone still in my hand, that I had a choice to make. I could continue to run from my fear, or I could face it.

So I swallowed hard and faced it.

And you know what? I survived the board meeting. Oh, I didn't have the smoothest delivery, but I prepared like crazy and I did my best. I chose to focus on doing excellent work rather than on the fear itself. It was a huge victory and a turning point in my life that opened new opportunities I could not have dreamed of.

Eleanor Roosevelt said, "You gain strength, courage, and confidence by every experience in which you really stop to look fear in the face. You are able to say to yourself, 'I have lived through this horror. I can take the next thing that comes along.' You must do the thing you think you cannot do."[3]

Fear is the single biggest force that will keep you from realizing your purpose in life.

We touched briefly on the fear of failure earlier, but so many other fears can hold us hostage too.

Fear of:

- Being embarrassed
- Public speaking
- Change
- Being hurt by others
- Being asked to do something you don't want to do
- Authority
- Failure
- Loving and being loved
- Heights
- Success
- Making mistakes
- Discovering uncomfortable truth
- Uncertainty
- The future
- Letting go of the past

The list could go on and on.

You see, the fun part of discovering your purpose is filling out questionnaires, trying new ideas, and drawing pretty pictures in the margins of this book. (I'm talking to you, creatives!)

The hard part, the scary part, is facing your fears, because it asks something of you. It asks you to trust the unknown, to step out of your comfort zone, and to *become*.

Discovering your purpose asks you to become brave.

This is exactly the posture you must take in order to move forward. You must face your fears.

READ

I prayed to the LORD, and he answered me.
   He freed me from all my fears.

PSALM 34:4

Don't be afraid, for I am with you.
   Don't be discouraged, for I am your God.
I will strengthen you and help you.
   I will hold you up with my victorious right hand.

ISAIAH 41:10

He will cover you with his feathers.
   He will shelter you with his wings.
   His faithful promises are your armor and protection.
Do not be afraid of the terrors of the night,
   nor the arrow that flies in the day.
Do not dread the disease that stalks in darkness,
   nor the disaster that strikes at midday.
Though a thousand fall at your side,
   though ten thousand are dying around you,
   these evils will not touch you.

PSALM 91:4-7

REFLECT

1. The spirit of fear is not from God. "For God has not given us a spirit of fear and timidity, but of power, love, and self-discipline," says 2 Timothy 1:7. When you feel fear start to paralyze you, remind yourself that you have been given the power to face it, the love to fight through it, and the self-discipline to overcome it.

2. Write a new script. Take a cue from top athletes who visualize themselves being successful. Put yourself into a different story by seeing yourself do the things you are afraid of, just like David, the biblical songwriter who is described as a man after God's own heart (1 Samuel 13:14), did in Psalm 23:4 (ESV): "Even though I walk through the valley of the shadow of death, I will fear no evil, for you are with me; your rod and your staff, they comfort me." He pictured himself walking safely through the thing he feared.

3. Don't wait for fear to go away. Take action in spite of it. "The LORD is with me; I will not be afraid. What can mere mortals do to me? The LORD is with me; he is my helper" (Psalm 118:6-7, NIV).

RESPOND

1. Write your new script here. Put yourself into the scenario you fear. What does it look like? Now, what are you doing differently, successfully? How does it feel? _____

   _____

   _____

   _____

   _____

   _____

   _____

   _____

2. Do one thing you're afraid of this week. Make that phone call, share something personal with someone you trust, sign up for a class, volunteer to teach, book a flight, or say yes to doing your best work even though you're fearful that you'll

be successful. Write what you will do here, along with a
completion date: _____

_____

_____

_____

_____

_____

_____

_____

3. Write out one of today's verses and apply it to your fear. You
   can do this in a prayer, naming your fear and asking God to
   help you break through the barrier that holds you hostage, or
   by simply speaking the verse aloud._____

_____

_____

_____

_____

_____

_____

Day Three
LEAN IN TO CURIOSITY

"I see God moving. . . . His coming is as brilliant as the sunrise."
HABAKKUK 3:18

"NANA! Look!" My two-year-old granddaughter, Ivy, stood in a rain puddle and held her hand out for me to see. In her palm was a small speckled stone, sparkling wet from the water she had pulled it from. I watched her turn over the small stone, studying its colors and shape with delight, before giving it to me for safekeeping. Then she stomped in the puddle with her rubber rain boots and laughed at the droplets that splashed everywhere, including onto me. To a toddler, every moment is a learning experience, such as "Splashing makes people laugh and chase you," otherwise known as "cause and effect."

Children's fascination with their world drives them to engage with their surroundings and make keen, often surprising observations as they go. They aren't afraid to ask questions such as "Why do cows sleep standing up?" and "Is the moon really made of cheese?" and "Why do my fingers have knees?" Their curiosity is limitless as they view things with young eyes, *new* eyes. Being with Ivy reminds me of all the wonder in the world around us, and how often we miss out on it in our busy adult lives. It's like being an adult and having to be productive have squeezed out any room for curiosity and the occasional outlandish question (of which I still have plenty).

The truth of the matter is that curiosity is the very quality that makes creative and productive work possible.

Albert Einstein is quoted as saying, "I have no special talent; I am only passionately curious." And it was out of that curiosity that the most important discoveries of the twentieth century were made, including the theory of relativity, the quantum theory of light, and the relationship between energy and mass. Today we have things such as cell phones, GPS, and nuclear energy as a result of Einstein's impassioned curiosity.

Leaning in to curiosity is our third guard tower posture.

It's an attitude that brings excitement and energy to our lives, and it comes with great news: *curiosity can be cultivated.*

Studies show that having an inquisitive mind has a host of positive benefits: better physical health, improved mental capabilities, and even deeper social relationships. People who are identified as "curious" tend to be happier and have a greater sense of life purpose, which is the thing we're after right here.[4]

Mark Twain reportedly said, "I have never let my schooling interfere with my education."[5] I love the sentiment behind it. Learning life skills, engaging your environment, and seeking out knowledge is a mind-set, not a degree program. It's found in listening, observing, looking for new experiences, and seeing things with new eyes. It's even found in asking outlandish questions!

READ

> One day Moses was tending the flock of his father-in-law,
> Jethro, the priest of Midian. He led the flock far into the
> wilderness and came to Sinai, the mountain of God. There
> the angel of the LORD appeared to him in a blazing fire
> from the middle of a bush. Moses stared in amazement.
> Though the bush was engulfed in flames, it didn't burn up.
> "This is amazing," Moses said to himself. "Why isn't that
> bush burning up? I must go see it."
>
> When the LORD saw Moses coming to take a closer look,
> God called to him from the middle of the bush, "Moses! Moses!"
>
> "Here I am!" Moses replied.
>
> EXODUS 3:1-4

REFLECT

Are you cultivating curiosity in your life? Consider these seven ways to foster curiosity:

1. Make time for play. Find activities that you enjoy, simply for the sake of enjoyment. Besides relieving stress, play frees your mind to think creatively and inquisitively.

2. Build your knowledge. The more you learn about a subject, the more engaged you become with it, and the more you'll *want* to know.

3. Try something new. Uncertainty about how an experience will turn out helps to heighten your senses and makes the activity

memorable. Tune in to how you respond to new situations—and then consider why you respond that way.

4. Become an observer. Examine the world around you by looking closely at details: colors, textures, sounds, smells, tastes. Use each of your senses to engage the experience.

5. Experience ho-hum activities in a new way. Look for ways to add interest by creating games out of tasks and chores you find boring. Change your setting, switch up your method, try working backward or upside down. Be conscious of your movements and thoughts as you do them.

6. Start a curiosity journal. Keep a running list of things you want to learn, books you'd like to read, places you'd like to go, and experiences you want to have. Record your progress by making observations, collecting mementos, or even drawing on the pages.

7. Be interested in other people. Develop the skill of asking good questions and learning about others. Everyone has a story to share, along with wisdom, experience, and different viewpoints. Become a listener!

RESPOND

Choose one of the seven strategies above to do today, and record it here:_____

_____

_____

_____

_____

_____

.... *Day Four* ....
EMBRACE YOUR STORY
. . . .

*"Even though the fig trees have no blossoms . . .
yet I will rejoice in the LORD!"*

HABAKKUK 3:18

WHEN I WROTE A MEMOIR in 2015, I planned to gloss over the part of my story that exposed the personal and financial struggles Tom and I endured during the years following the recession of 2008. Our art business had all but tanked as the market for our services disappeared almost overnight. We felt like such failures, and we could point to any number of things we could have done differently, any number of ways we should have handled it better. The embarrassment of failing in that one thing we thought we were *supposed* to do made me withdraw from friendships and hold people at arm's length. Outwardly, we did a pretty good job maintaining a bootstrap-but-successful image of entrepreneurs, but the stress *inside* was almost unbearable at times. I hoped no one would ever know the truth.

Right in the middle of our struggle, a stray donkey arrived on our driveway—as I mentioned in week two—and provided some welcome relief to our situation through his entertaining antics. I thought that writing a humorous story about this donkey would make for a fun, enjoyable book. *Of course it would! Do it, Rachel! It will be awesome! You can leave out the embarrassing parts!*

However, when I actually sat down to write my story, I knew in my heart that I could not avoid the truth of everything that had happened. I realized that if I was to write a story worth reading, I would have to own it. I'd have to embrace the parts that caused me shame, just as much as the parts I was proudest of. It was a difficult and painful posture to assume. But the amazing thing is that in doing it, I learned an incredible lesson: the shame of the past only has power as long as it stays hidden.

As hard as it may be, exposing the truth sets us free. Sharing my story brought a level of joy I had not thought possible and helped me see how I'd let the fear of being fully known control so much of my life. I was astounded by the number of people who said, "Me too," and then shared *their* stories with me. Being honest paved a way for healing—both for me and for others.

Our *stories* are what make us human. They are what give meaning and context to who we are and what we do. And equally important, they allow us to connect powerfully with other people through the bridge of vulnerability. As long as we hide behind a veneer of having it all together, we will never know true intimacy with others or the true freedom to bloom into our best selves.

We cannot fully live out our life purpose until we embrace our own stories.

This means that we must face the parts of our lives we don't like—the trauma, the hardships, the painful experiences, the things that we are ashamed of—and recognize that they hold us hostage. Breaking free can only happen when we choose to own them. It's when we can say:

Yes, this happened to me.

Yes, I did this.

Yes, I blew it.

Yes, I was hurt.

Yes, I was abandoned.

Yes, I am afraid.

Those moments of our lives that are deeply personal and private are some of the most powerful in shaping who we are and why we do the things we do. When we avoid our past or situations that make us feel ashamed, we are allowing those things to hold us back from becoming whole. We can't grow into our true purpose in life.

Embracing our stories does not mean that we continue to live *in* them, stuck for all time. Instead, it means that we bring them out into the light of truth, we become willing to tell them, and we allow them to bring light and life to the world.

Every moment of your life is uniquely yours.

Every moment can be a catalyst for healing.

Every moment can be reclaimed through God's love.

Every moment can be redeemed for God's purposes.

READ

Read John 4:1-42—the account of the woman at the well, someone whose story changed an entire town.

REFLECT

Your story is what makes you uniquely *you*. There is no one else like you in this world. Your experiences, your past, your successes, your failures, your struggles—all of it is part of what makes you who you are.

The world needs your story. Embrace it.

RESPOND

1. If your story was written in book form, what would be the theme of the narrative?_____

_____

_____

_____

_____

2. What parts of your story are you ashamed of? _____

_____

_____

_____

_____

_____

_____

3. What parts of your life story are you proud of? _____

_____

_____

_____

_____

_____

4. If you've ever shared your story with another person, what was the response? Was it positive or negative? _____

_____

_____

_____

_____

_____

5. Can you think of ways your story could positively impact the world? _____

_____

_____

_____

_____

_____

.... *Day Five* ....
REACH OUT TO FRIENDSHIPS

. . . .

"You went out . . . to save your anointed ones."
HABAKKUK 3:13

STANDING IN THE WATCHTOWER, scanning the horizon and watching for signs, gives Habakkuk plenty of time to think. He shifts his weight and adjusts his shoulders. He squints at some movement out to the west, all his senses heightened and ready. *Ah, just some shepherds moving their herds.* He rubs his chin thoughtfully. Ordinarily, he'd be down in the Temple, studying sacred scrolls or learning a new music piece for the next festival, not up here by himself. For a moment, a wave of loneliness hits him, but then he remembers his teammates.

He glances at the guards on post (one gives him a thumbs-up sign), then lets his gaze wander to the gatekeepers, the message runners, and the assistants standing by with water and food to help him keep his strength up. He hears the sounds of the Temple musicians, singing their prayers and calling out their praises to God, and that's when he feels revived.

Habakkuk knows that his mission up in the tower is only made possible by a large group of supportive people who know he's on an important assignment. His friends and coworkers have not only picked up the slack left by his absence, they've encouraged him to follow the leading that God has given him. His mentors, the ones who first saw his prophetic gifts as a young man, nodded their approval at him as he hurried to the tower to wait for his assignment.

At least, that's how *I* envision it.

The short pages of the book of Habakkuk really don't say how it happened, but if I know anything about how God works, it's that it is always through a network of people.

Your best work, your purpose-filled life-work, will be directly correlated with the relationships you are a part of.

It makes me think of Jesus and how He surrounded Himself with a circle of people to accomplish the greatest work in the history of the world. His example of investing in a small group of friends inspires us to think about purpose in terms of relationships. Jesus and His friends spent time together. They shared experiences. Jesus mentored these people over meals, as they traveled, and as they did life with one another. And after He was gone, His followers depended on each other as they continued to carry out their divine purpose.

They spurred one another on to keep living for something greater than themselves, and in so doing, they changed the world.

Do you want to fast-track discovering and living your purpose?

Reach out to other people. Build relationships.

Live in this posture.

Reach out to people who are living *their* purpose. Find them, befriend them, observe them, and . . . help *them* keep accomplishing their purpose.

But don't stop there.

Hold out your hands to those coming along behind you—those who are in need of encouragement. Find them, befriend them, observe them, and . . . help *them* accomplish their purposes too.

Building relationships is not about networking in a self-serving sense. It's all about seeking out and deepening *friendships*. It's about bringing value to others, with no expectation of what you'll receive in return. It's about taking an active interest in, sacrificing for, and loving others.

The right posture, the posture of reaching out, will put you smack-dab in the middle of all kinds of goodness. It is like a soup of emotional and physical well-being.[6] Best of all, God can do what He likes to do: make His purposes known, and give you the support system to go out and accomplish them.

READ

There is no greater love than to lay down one's life for one's friends.   JOHN 15:13

Therefore I, a prisoner for serving the Lord, beg you to lead a life worthy of your calling, for you have been called by God. Always be humble and gentle. Be patient with each other, making allowance for each other's faults because of your love. Make every effort to keep yourselves united in the Spirit, binding yourselves together with peace.   EPHESIANS 4:1-3

REFLECT

Friendships are part of the foundation for purposeful living. As you reach out to others in positive ways, good things naturally happen:

your physical and emotional health is improved, your sense of well-being is enhanced, and your sense of purpose grows.

Dale Carnegie said in his bestselling book *How to Win Friends and Influence People*, "You can make more friends in two months by becoming interested in other people than you can in two years by trying to get other people interested in you."[7]

And C. S. Lewis put it well: "The next best thing to being wise oneself is to live in a circle of those who are."[8]

RESPOND

1. Do you have a circle of friends and acquaintances who are positive influences in your life? Are there people who consistently model purposeful living? Write three names here:

   _____

   _____

   _____

2. List one specific thing you can do for each of these friends this week. _____

   _____

   _____

   _____

   _____

   _____

   _____

3. Name three people who are positively affected by *your* life—those for whom you model purposeful or wise living: _____

   _____

   _____

   _____

4. List one specific thing you can do for each of these friends this
    week. _____

    _____

    _____

    _____

    _____

    _____

    _____

5. Name one person you admire but don't know personally. List
    one way you can reach out. _____

    _____

    _____

    _____

    _____

    _____

    _____

Week Five
PURPOSEFUL IN THE WAIT

. . . .

*"He does have surprising, secret purposes. I open a Bible,
and His plans, startling, lie there barefaced."*

ANN VOSKAMP

HABAKKUK VOICED his honest prayers to God; then he climbed and positioned himself in the watchtower, where he stood poised for God's answer. Now that answer finally arrives in the form of a vision. Hooray!

So . . . what happens next?

Like Habakkuk, we've been looking for clarity. We've jotted down ideas, we've answered questions, we've put ourselves in position to hear from God. But what happens when we *do* hear? What happens when we have a clear (or at least better) understanding of what our purpose is? Does that mean it will happen immediately?

Sometimes it does.

And sometimes, the vision is for a future time, and get this—we are instructed to wait for it.

What? Wait? *No!*

That's not what we want to hear. We would much rather go, and do, and be, and conquer! It's time to accomplish stuff. Let's get this show on the road.

And yet, in almost every person's life, there will be periods of waiting. There will be seasons of feeling like you're on hold. Waiting is such a predictable occurrence that it's like it's built into the process of purpose. Almost like waiting is part of the whole plan. Like it's "Ready, get set, . . . wait!"

Waiting, at some point, is inevitable.

Well, if waiting is an unavoidable part of the process of purpose, it seems like it's something we should take a look at. Because waiting can be either a waste of time or an investment of time. It can be a time of languishing or a time of flourishing.

Waiting can be productive, and it can be useful if we have the right perspective on it.

This week, we are going to spend some time talking about what to do in the wait. If you feel that your dream or vision for your life is on hold, then just . . . well, hold on. This is your week.

Day One
TRUST GOD'S TIMING

"If it seems slow in coming . . ."

HABAKKUK 2:3

WHEN I WAS TWENTY YEARS OLD, I knew I was born to write a book. I had a deep burning in my soul to put my words on paper and share my story with the world. So, I announced to my husband of one year that I would write that book, starting right then and there.

I set up our typewriter, positioned a lamp, made a pot of coffee, and settled in a chair at the desk. I tapped out my first sentence: "I was born on a rainy morning in Seattle."

And . . . that's where my inspiration ceased.

After rewriting my opening line several times, I decided to shelve my story for a few days so I could think about it a little more. Well, days turned into weeks, then months, then whole years. Occasionally, I would think about my attempt at writing (with a bit of embarrassment) and still feel that burning, only now it was more like a sad little ember, buried so deep I could hardly find it. My dream of writing seemed like a fanciful illusion.

Years later—thirty, to be exact—the ember took flame once again, and suddenly I had a book to write. This time it was different. I actually *had* a story to tell. All those years of waiting were for a purpose. They were meant for me to grow up and live and have experiences that would deepen me. I had to have some big failures under my belt, as well as a few successes, in order for my purpose to be fully realized. That dream of writing *had* to wait. It had to sit on the back burner while God accomplished other important things in my life.

My vision was for a future time, but God was working *in my present all along* to make it come about.

Back in the first chapter of Habakkuk, God addresses this very idea. It's a little gem in verse 5.

> Look around at the nations;
>   look and be amazed!
> *For I am doing something in your own day,*
>   something you wouldn't believe
>   even if someone told you about it.
> HABAKKUK 1:5, EMPHASIS ADDED

Listen. All this talk about waiting for a vision to arrive. All this talk about the vision being for a future time. All this focus on preparing and positioning. It's all good. It's all necessary. But it's easy to miss this very important detail:

God is working now. Today. Even when we don't see it.

God has a timetable for our lives that may seem out of touch with our fast-paced world. We are so accustomed to quick results and instant gratification that we rarely have to wait on anything anymore. I mean, I'm usually standing by the microwave, telling it to hurry and heat my food so I can gulp it down and get to the next thing on my to-do list. It's no wonder I can't handle an answer like "It's going to be a while, honey."

But here's the thing: I can trust that God's purpose is already under way in my life. He is not in a hurry, and He won't rush the process to satisfy my demands. He will bring everything to fruition at just the right time.

Are you frustrated with the wait? Do you feel like nothing is happening?

You're not alone. The Bible is filled with stories of people who found themselves waiting: people like Joseph, who endured being sold into slavery by his own brothers, being imprisoned, and then working his way to a position of power so that he could save nations (including his family) from famine. People like Moses, who waited forty years in exile before leading his people out of Egypt. People like Anna, a widow who stayed at the Temple day and night to worship God and after years of waiting saw the baby Messiah. The list could go on. God took His time to put all the pieces into place.

My point is this: Waiting is *part* of God's plan. It's His MO. And if you find yourself in a period of waiting, rest assured that you're not outside of God's will. You haven't missed the boat. You haven't wandered away from His purposes.

You're *exactly* where you're supposed to be, and you can trust Him.

READ

"I am Joseph!" he said to his brothers. "Is my father still alive?" But his brothers were speechless! They were stunned to realize that Joseph was standing there in front of them.

"Please, come closer," he said to them. So they came closer. And he said again, "I am Joseph, your brother, whom you sold into slavery in Egypt. But don't be upset, and don't be angry with yourselves for selling me to this place. It was God who sent me here ahead of you to preserve your lives. This famine that has ravaged the land for two years will last five more years, and there will be neither plowing nor harvesting. God has sent me ahead of you to keep you and your families alive and to preserve many survivors. So it was God who sent me here, not you! And he is the one who made me an adviser to Pharaoh—the manager of his entire palace and the governor of all Egypt." GENESIS 45:3-8

(You can read the entire story of Joseph in Genesis 37–50.)

REFLECT

In the passage above, Joseph tells the end of the story to his brothers. But imagine how he might have felt in the middle of the story, when he was sold into slavery, or when he spent time in prison, long before he became an adviser to Pharaoh. Do you think he may have felt forgotten? What would you have told him?

RESPOND

1. Assuming you are in the middle of your story, what would you tell yourself? How would you encourage yourself to trust God?

_____

_____

_____

_____

_____

_____

We know that God causes everything to work together for
the good of those who love God and are called according to
his purpose for them.   ROMANS 8:28

Now that you've read it, write Romans 8:28 out by hand on a
three-by-five-inch card (or Post-it Note). Place it where you will
see it each day, and remind yourself that even waiting is part of
the "everything" God is working together for good.

2. List the things you are learning from having to wait._____

_____

_____

_____

_____

_____

_____

3. Pick one of the things and write a sentence about how it might
be valuable to you *in the future.*_____

_____

_____

_____

_____

_____

_____

Day Two
WRITE IT DOWN

"Write my answer . . ."

HABAKKUK 2:2

RECENTLY, I STUMBLED across an old journal of mine that had been tucked away in a dresser drawer. I have a lot of journals, most of them filled with blank pages. Time after time, I've started writing in a new book with great enthusiasm and then left it to collect dust by my bedside. I'm an inconsistent journaler, to say the least. Still, as I looked through the pages, a flood of memories came back, spurred by some of my life's best and worst moments that had been jotted down. My favorite entries are the ones from everyday life. One such page took me back in time to when our third child was an infant. I wrote a timeline of my day: changing diapers, nursing, folding laundry, picking up the older kids from school, nursing, changing diapers, making dinner, helping with homework, nursing, changing diapers, overseeing bedtime. I finished my list with a brief commentary: "Good day. Exhausted."

I remembered why there are so many blank pages in the journal after that. I was too tired to write anything! I sat on the edge of the bed with the journal in my hands and realized how much of the past I'd forgotten. Without that hastily scribbled notation, I would even have forgotten *that* day. Seeing the words on the page made my history come alive, and it made me appreciate just how far we'd come as a family.

I flipped to the front of the book to find another entry from years earlier. This one caught me by surprise and instantly formed a lump in my throat: "I want to be the best mom I can be."

It was a simple sentence that summed up my goal (and hopes) in that season of life, one that powerfully propelled me through the hard days. The ink on the page had faded a bit, but the message behind it still had an impact on me, all these years later.

The written word is powerful.

Maybe that's why God's vision for Habakkuk began with this instruction: "Write my answer plainly on tablets."

He knew that Habakkuk and all of His people would need a permanent record that would not be forgotten in the tumultuous times to come. The written word would be preserved, not just for the people experiencing the situation in real time, but for all time—which is why we have it today. I'm so glad Habakkuk not only wrote the vision down but added his own poetic touch to the message with the third chapter. He put his heart into it, along with all his emotions, and created a compelling, unforgettable work.

What can we learn from this as we choose to live lives of purpose?

I think you're already a step ahead of me. Simply this: Write out what's on your heart. Keep a record. And just as important, *write out your goals.*

Stated, written goals create a potent force for action to take place.

It's what you've been doing (hopefully!) throughout our time together. You've been taking notes, jotting ideas, filling in blanks . . . and each time you do, you are underscoring the message that this is *important work*. This is what you are applying yourself to. You are heading somewhere, and you are discovering your purpose in the process. This is what turns seasons of waiting into seasons of preparation. Purposeful waiting.

"The secret to accomplishing what matters most to you is committing your goals to writing," says Michael Hyatt, author of *Living Forward: A Proven Plan to Stop Drifting and Get the Life You Want*.[9]

Want to stand out from the rest of the world? Simply write down your goals. Most people never get that far. As a result, most people never accomplish the things that are important to them. Turn your dreams into goals by writing them down.

READ

Commit your actions to the LORD,
　　and your plans will succeed.
PROVERBS 16:3

Having carefully investigated everything from the beginning,
I also have decided to write an accurate account for you,
most honorable Theophilus.　LUKE 1:3

This is what the LORD, the God of Israel, says: Write down
for the record everything I have said to you, Jeremiah.
JEREMIAH 30:2

Joshua recorded these things in the Book of God's
Instructions. As a reminder of their agreement, he took a
huge stone and rolled it beneath the terebinth tree beside the
Tabernacle of the LORD.　JOSHUA 24:26

REFLECT

Here are five practical reasons to write down your goals.

1. It helps you clarify what is important to you.

2. It gives you a significantly better chance of accomplishing them. (More about that in day four's reflection.)

3. It helps you quantify them.

4. It helps your unconscious brain begin to actively consider how to make them happen—through people, knowledge, and resources.

5. It helps you imagine what it will feel like to accomplish them.

RESPOND

1. Look back through your notes and filled-in pages in this work-book. As you review the previous weeks' lessons, put your ideas, dreams, and passions into actual goals . . . and into writing on the lines provided. Keep it simple by focusing on those goals that have to do with your purpose and passion. _____

    _____

    _____

    _____

    _____

    _____

    _____

2. Visualize what it will feel like to accomplish them.

Day Three
BE CLEAR

". . . plainly on tablets."

HABAKKUK 2:2

A FEW YEARS AGO, our daughter had a wish: to have her autumn wedding on our property. It was a lovely idea, but we knew it would be a lot of work to pull off an outdoor event for 250 people. Once a date was set, we sat down with notebooks and began making lists of everything that would need to be done. Our goal was to have a beautiful, memorable event that was stress-free (or at least stress-*minimal*).

Everything—from planting grass and watering it three times a day for six weeks in the middle of a drought, to clearing out the barn for a reception, to turning a pasture into a parking area—had to be thought through and put on a calendar. With so many details involved, we found ourselves continually losing track of what needed to be done and when.

Finally, we created a large flowchart on a wall of our house. We used a Sharpie and index cards to write out each task, and we organized it all by taping the cards to the wall so that every family member knew what his or her responsibilities were. If there were any questions, we could simply look at the wall and see exactly what was supposed to happen.

The wedding and reception came off beautifully. The November day was glorious, and except for a couple of minor hiccups (such as the wind blowing the arch of flowers over just before the ceremony), the whole event was incredible. Everyone had a great time, and few people realized the months of work that went into making it look easy.

A goal and a clear plan made our daughter's wish possible.

It's a small example of the kind of thing Habakkuk mentions here:

Write my answer plainly on tablets,
> so that a runner can carry the correct message to others.

HABAKKUK 2:2

The word *tablet* may make you think of your iPad, but in this case it was more likely a large piece of wood or parchment that Habakkuk would have written on in big letters and posted in a public place so that people could read the message as they passed by. It was almost like an ancient PowerPoint presentation: words on giant screens, clearly visible from a distance.

That's how clear God wanted His vision to be.

Habakkuk was to take God's message and not only write it in an understandable way, but write it *big*, and post it as a visible reminder so that action would take place.

Today (and tomorrow), I want us to expand on yesterday's concept of writing things down and take our assignment of written goals a step further. See, it's tempting to write out a personal vision or goal in a notebook, then close the pages and forget about it, especially when we feel like we're in a season of waiting. Writing is a great first step, but it needs something more in order to be effective.

Every goal needs a clear plan.

Otherwise, it's just a fanciful wish.

READ

Good planning and hard work lead to prosperity,
   but hasty shortcuts lead to poverty.

PROVERBS 21:5

Joseph responded . . . "Therefore, Pharaoh should find an intelligent and wise man and put him in charge of the entire land of Egypt. Then Pharaoh should appoint supervisors over the land and let them collect one-fifth of all the crops during the seven good years. Have them gather all the food produced in the good years that are just ahead and bring it to Pharaoh's storehouses. Store it away, and guard it so there will be food in the cities. That way there will be enough to eat when the seven years of famine come to the land of Egypt. Otherwise this famine will destroy the land."

Joseph's suggestions were well received by Pharaoh and his officials. So Pharaoh asked his officials, "Can we find anyone else like this man so obviously filled with the spirit of God?" Then Pharaoh said to Joseph, "Since God has revealed the meaning of the dreams to you, clearly no one else is as intelligent or wise as you are. You will be in charge of my court, and all my people will take orders from you. Only I, sitting on my throne, will have a rank higher than yours." GENESIS 41:25, 33-40

REFLECT

In the story above, Joseph had just interpreted two troubling dreams that Pharaoh had. Then he offered a good plan for dealing with the impending famine. Joseph's wise planning created a job opening for him in Pharaoh's court.

Some people are afraid to set goals because they feel they will fail. Studies show that resolutions (such as New Year's resolutions) are likely to fail, but goals with actionable steps to achieving them have a much higher success rate. As Antoine de Saint-Exupéry is credited with saying, "A goal without a plan is just a wish."

RESPOND

Perhaps you've heard of SMART goal setting.[10] This is a simple acronym to turn goals into realities. SMART goals are *specific* (I will learn to play the guitar), *measurable* (I will be able to play one song well), *attainable* (I will take lessons once a week), *relevant* (so I can play along with my daughter), and *time-bound* (by the spring recital).

Take one of your goals from yesterday's assignment and fill in the following:

S	Specific: What is my goal?	
M	Measurable: How will I know it's complete?	
A	Attainable: How can it be accomplished?	
R	Relevant: Why is it worth doing?	
T	Time-bound: When will it be accomplished?	

.... *Day Four* ....
BE ACCOUNTABLE

. . . .

". . . so that a runner can carry the correct message to others."

HABAKKUK 2:2

"SEE YOU WEDNESDAY MORNING, BRIGHT AND EARLY!" My friend Bridgette gave me a sweaty hug and turned to walk up her driveway. The sticky summer morning had left both of us dripping with perspiration from our two-mile walk around our rural neighborhood. Walking—in July . . . in Texas—must be done early, or the heat and humidity just might kill you.

My neighbor and I both have crazy schedules. As work-from-home business owners who juggle a variety of projects, it's hard to have fixed times to exercise. I've dropped out of more Zumba and yoga classes than I care to admit "on account of my schedule." At least that's what I like to tell myself.

The real truth is, I don't like to sweat. (Can I get a high five here?)

Good thing Bridgette can see right through my reasons, er, excuses.

She is even busier than I am. So rather than having a set day and time to meet, the best we can do is take each week as it comes, finding two or three mornings that will work for both of us. Sometimes a text will light up my phone at night, letting me know she's available the next morning and asking if I can walk.

Though often hit-and-miss, we keep up with it because we don't want to let the other person down. Honestly, we both know that if left on my own, I'd always choose an extra half hour of sleep over exercising, and left on *her* own, she'd do the same. Knowing that Bridgette will be waiting for me at the mailbox in the morning makes me put my feet on the floor and get ready, even if it means I'm going to have to sweat a little bit.

Accountability does that.

> *Accountability is a secret weapon for success when it comes to achieving goals and dreams.*

Knowing that someone may check on your progress is an amazing motivator! In fact, many a plan—even with a specific, measurable, attainable, relevant, and timely goal—suffers defeat because of one small detail: lack of accountability.

I love that Habakkuk put the words of his vision on display for all the world to see. Talk about being held accountable! Anyone could read his words and make a judgment on whether or not they were true. Anyone could question his motivation, his purpose, and his ability to hear from God simply because he laid it out there.

Habakkuk put himself in a vulnerable position.

Let's face it. Telling your vision to others can be scary.

Habakkuk could have kept it under wraps. That way, if nothing came to pass, no one would be the wiser. *He could have saved himself so much embarrassment.*

But he didn't. He proclaimed it.

Something happens when we give voice to our dreams, when we tell others about them. They are taken from the secret world of wishes, and they get solidified in a concrete form of reality. They become actual *things*. *Things that we are now accountable for.*

Yes, it's scary. It feels risky.

When you share your vision or your goals with others, there is the possibility of criticism. You might be questioned about your motivation, or your judgment, or your sheer audacity. The possibility of embarrassment feels huge.

It takes some bravery.

Because what if you fail?

Let me encourage you today. Don't let fear of being embarrassed keep you from making yourself accountable. You are far more likely to experience failure if you do *not* share your dreams than if you do share them. Sharing your goals and being accountable is like adding rocket fuel to your passion. You instantly become invested in your dreams, and that invites others to invest also. That investment will get you out of bed in the morning, even if you have to sweat a little bit.

READ

Plans go wrong for lack of advice;
    many advisers bring success.
PROVERBS 15:22

As iron sharpens iron,
    so a friend sharpens a friend.
PROVERBS 27:17

A person standing alone can be attacked and defeated, but two can stand back-to-back and conquer. Three are even better, for a triple-braided cord is not easily broken.
ECCLESIASTES 4:12

REFLECT

Remember me saying in day two's reflection that writing down your goals "gives you a significantly better chance of accomplishing them"? This was one of the key conclusions of a study conducted by clinical psychologist and professor Gail Matthews at Dominican University of California. The study found that individuals with written goals and accountability achieved approximately 33 percent more of their goals than those who had not put them into writing. In addition, individuals who made a public commitment to their goals and were held accountable to those goals were substantially more likely to accomplish them.[11]

Now, be honest with yourself. What would prevent you from sharing your goals with someone?

RESPOND

Ask a trusted friend if you can share one of your goals with her. Tell her that you will check in with her once a week for the next five weeks to let her know your progress. This will not require anything of your friend except to receive your progress reports.

My friend is: _____

_____

My goal is: _____

_____

_____

Write your goal out on a piece of paper and place it in a public place, such as on the refrigerator door. At the bottom, include a line to write in the date when the goal is completed.

Day Five
BE PATIENT, BUT NOT PARKED

". . . wait patiently . . ."
HABAKKUK 2:3

MY FRIEND BEVERLY is someone I really admire. As a university admissions officer, she has a busy, demanding job that includes a lot of travel. She juggles a schedule that would intimidate the best of us, yet she always seems calm in the midst of it. I met Beverly when we both volunteered to be on a creative team for a nonprofit organization, and we ended up running the merchandise tables together. After one of the recent events, we sat down to rub our tired feet and catch our breath. She told me about a young lady whom she had been helping to find direction in her life.

"Have you always known that helping people was your purpose?" I asked her.

Beverly paused for a moment. "When I was a young woman I thought that I'd go off and do something big and grandiose in the world. I had such great passion for being a world-changer. I thought I'd be speaking to thousands and starting my own organization to teach people life skills. Instead, I found myself in the corporate world, and while I was waiting for that important ministry opportunity to show up, I ended up staying there. For every job I've had, there has always been something extra for me to be a part of. There have been people whom I otherwise would never have met that I can help. Sometimes it's in small ways, like saying a prayer with them, and other times it's more than that. I just find that God always puts things in front of me to do."

Then she said, "I guess the answer to your question is yes. I always knew I wanted to help people, and I thought I knew what that would look like. I'm living my purpose, and it's more exciting than I could have imagined."

Beverly is onto something.

When she was waiting for her big opportunity to show up, she could have decided that world-changing was not for her. She could have simply worked at her job, banked her paycheck, and enjoyed her two-week vacations. Instead, she looks for opportunities to put her skills and talents to use. She finds young people who can use a helping hand and mentors them. She reaches out to people. Beverly didn't let the wait keep her sidelined. She's found ways to keep moving toward her purpose, and in the process she's found fulfillment and joy.

Waiting is inevitable, remember? Perhaps you find yourself in an unfulfilling job, or you spend your days doing work that seems to have nothing to do with your personal goals or purpose. Or maybe you're in the midst of mastering a skill or getting a degree, and nothing seems to be happening to put it to the kind of use you thought it should be. You're waiting for an opportunity to arrive that will change everything.

"If it seems slow in coming, wait patiently" is God's message in Habakkuk 2:3.

Patient waiting does not mean passive waiting.

It does not mean that you're stuck at home waiting for the telephone to ring. Patient waiting means trusting that God's timing is best, and then realizing that there is always something to do in the present. He puts opportunities in your path that will not only equip you for the future but are important *here and now*. Your job is to choose to do something with them.

Don't know what to do while you wait? Find someone whom you can help. Google organizations where you can serve. Offer your expertise on a project that needs your skill set. Take the time to prepare: further your education, get job or vocational training, find a mentor. Use this time to try new things as you "lean in to curiosity" as we talked about last week.

READ

Teach us to number our days,
    that we may gain a heart of wisdom.

PSALM 90:12, NIV

He gives power to the faint,
    and to him who has no might he increases strength.
Even youths shall faint and be weary,
    and young men shall fall exhausted;
but they who wait for the LORD shall renew
      their strength;
    they shall mount up with wings like eagles;
they shall run and not be weary;
    they shall walk and not faint.

ISAIAH 40:29-31, ESV

Trust in the LORD and do good.

PSALM 37:3

REFLECT

One of my favorite quotes of all time is "Opportunity favors the prepared." Although no one knows who actually said it, I've personally experienced what it means. I've had amazing opportunities come my way that I've been unprepared for, and as a result, I've missed out on them. *Oh, the heartbreak!* It's spurred me on to hone my creative crafts during my downtime, sharpen my professional skills through practice and seminars, and connect with others in my field.

We are all given the same amount of time . . . it's just that some people do great things with theirs. Rather than thinking about "someday," let's make today count.

RESPOND

Are you waiting for an opportunity to come your way? Don't shift into park and take a nap! Activate your purpose by doing three new things this week. Here are some ideas to get you started, but don't limit yourself to mine. You know what needs to be on your list.

- Call one new friend.
- Volunteer for something outside your comfort zone.
- Sign up for an art class (or music class, or accounting class, or continuing education class).
- Read a book in a genre you don't normally choose.
- Drive a different route home from work or running errands. Take your time and note new places to explore.
- Visit a museum and learn something you didn't know about our world.

- Step up your goal plans by challenging yourself with a short deadline.
- Send a thank-you note to someone you appreciate.
- Join a group at church or a local community center.
- Review your bucket list and check one thing off.

Write your three activities here, with their completion dates:

Activity	Date
1)	
2)	
3)	

Week Six
PROMISED FOR GOD'S GLORY

· ·

"The Present is the point at which time touches eternity."
C. S. LEWIS

CAN YOU BELIEVE that this is our last week? We started out by comparing our activities together to an underpainting—the idea that we would be roughing in a composition in loose, broad strokes. Each day, I've presented ideas and questions to help jump-start your creativity and inspire your thinking, because only *you* can finish the painting that will become the masterpiece of your life. No one can give you an exact picture of what your life purpose should be, and to be perfectly honest, I think it's supposed to be that way. As you dip your paintbrush into all the colors and experiences of your life, you'll get to watch your purpose unfold in all its glory. I believe God is bringing about something amazing for you!

This week is all about encouragement for your journey. Throughout your life, you will write and rewrite your goals and dreams scores of times as new information challenges you to grow and change. But some things will always remain constant, and there are five important keys I want to share with you. These concepts are a filter through which you'll view your circumstances, your direction, and your decisions. They describe ways to live so that each day is filled with purpose, even if you're not sure exactly how it will unfold.

Day One
LIVE IN THE PROMISE

"This vision . . . will surely take place. It will not be delayed."

HABAKKUK 2:3-4

"I PROMISE I WON'T LET GO," my father-in-law assured our oldest daughter, Lauren, who was four at the time. They were at the community swimming pool, which sparkled under the summer sun, and Lauren sat on the first step, the water lapping around her small body. Her grandpa had been helping her learn how to swim, and now it was time to attempt it without arm floaties. She looked nervously at all the bigger kids who were splashing and roughhousing in the water nearby, and her eyes filled with tears.

"But I'm scared!" she said.

Grandpa moved in front of her and held out his arms. "I'll hold you up," he said, "and I won't let anyone splash you."

Lauren hesitated for another moment. Then she thought about how Grandpa had shown her how to kick her legs and move her arms. He had been patient with her, and he had never let anything frightening happen to her during the previous days' lessons. With a glance at the other kids, she lowered herself to the next step. The water was now chest deep, and her arms reached forward.

"I'm right here, I promise," Grandpa's voice reassured her.

With that, Lauren pushed off the step and into his waiting arms. He gently maneuvered her around so that his hands held her tummy and her arms and legs had freedom to move. She kicked as hard as she could, while he moved right along with her forward motion. As promised, he did not let go of her . . . until she gave him permission to do so. Then, of course, she took off on her own, all smiles and giggles.

Lauren learned how to swim that day, and she also learned that she could trust her grandpa to do just what he said he would. He didn't trick her into *thinking* he'd hold her up and then let go and allow her to sink. He didn't push her to do more than she was ready for. He promised to hold her up until she was ready to swim without help, and that's exactly what he did.

As adults, we often wish we had a kindly grandpa at our side 24-7 to reassure us during those scary moments of life. *Is it going to be okay? Am I going to make it? Will you hold me up?* We need someone who can promise to hold us steady until we are ready to make it on our own.

I'm so glad that we have a God who does even more than that for us. The Bible reveals a loving God who promises that we can trust Him, no matter what we face. Many people turn to the Bible to find out how to get to heaven when they die, but they don't realize that it's also full of assurances for the life they are living now. There are promises for every situation we may face, and God wants us to know that He's got the power to fulfill all of them.

Our little book of Habakkuk rolls out God's promise for the vision that seems to take so long to get here:

"It will surely take place. It will not be delayed" (2:3).

No matter how long it takes, it will happen. You can count on it. It won't take one minute longer than is necessary.

God's purposes for you will surely come. Right on time.

This is the eternal God, all-powerful and all-seeing, who reassures us through the words in the Bible that He is *for us.* He loves us and will not leave us without His presence and power, or His wisdom and strength. As you wait on Him for direction, or for that dream to be fulfilled, He is watching over you every moment. He *will* cause it to come about.

Don't lose heart. Don't worry. Don't be afraid.

God's got you. He won't let go. *Promise.*

READ

The LORD will guide you continually,
   giving you water when you are dry
   and restoring your strength.
You will be like a well-watered garden,
   like an ever-flowing spring.

ISAIAH 58:11

REFLECT

Here are fifteen promises from God to remember as you discover your purpose and calling.

1. Your vision will surely come. (Habakkuk 2:3)
2. He will never leave you. (Deuteronomy 31:6)
3. God delights in every detail of your life. (Psalm 37:23)

4. Nothing separates you from His love. (Romans 8:38-39)

5. God works all things out for good. (Romans 8:28)

6. He cares for you. (1 Peter 5:7)

7. He gives you strength. (Isaiah 41:10)

8. He gives you rest. (Matthew 11:29)

9. He gives you power, love, and self-discipline. (2 Timothy 1:7)

10. He gives you the desires of your heart. (Psalm 37:4)

11. God gives you guidance. (Psalm 32:8)

12. He answers prayer. (Jeremiah 33:3)

13. He will help you. (Psalm 37:5)

14. He will provide for your needs. (Matthew 6:25-30)

15. He will fulfill His purpose for you. (Psalm 138:8)

RESPOND

1. Write out one of the promise verses above, and work on memorizing it. _____

   _____

   _____

2. How does knowing God keeps His promises help you *today?*

   _____

   _____

   _____

   _____

3. What will you do differently, knowing that God holds all things in His hands? _____

   _____

   _____

   _____

   _____

   _____

4. What specific promises are you holding in your heart? _____

_____

_____

_____

_____

_____

_____

Day Two
LIVE HUMBLY

*"Look at the proud! They trust in themselves,
and their lives are crooked."*

HABAKKUK 2:4

MY HUSBAND MOTIONED for me to roll down the driver's-side window so he could give me a few instructions on how to drive our Suburban through the mud. Flooding rains had left our driveway impassable, and I needed to take an alternate route through our neighbor's muddy pasture to get to the road.

I held my hand up to stop him midsentence.

"Yeah. I've got this," I said, annoyed that Tom thought I needed his help navigating the vehicle. *I'm an excellent driver and don't need your tips*, I thought as I closed the window on him. I may or may not have given him the stink eye.

"Okay, I'll walk up ahead and help direct you," he responded with a tap on the hood and a thumbs-up.

With my foot gently pressing the gas pedal, I slowly but steadily made my way through the gate and into the grassy area, which was on an incline.

And that's where I ran into problems.

The saturated earth immediately gave way beneath the heavy Suburban, and I felt the back tires begin to slip. The rear of the truck rotated to the left, despite my effort to keep moving forward. Mud flew in all directions, and the wheels sank into deep grooves.

I threw the truck into park and slouched in defeat. It had only taken seconds for me to fail. Tom sauntered back to the window and said, "May I help you now?" He had the nerve to be smiling at me.

"You were just up there humoring me, weren't you?" I asked, unbuckling my seat belt and opening the door.

He shrugged. "Yeah, I knew you'd get stuck."

Fortunately, the only thing hurt that day was my pride as I stood to the side and watched the expert begin to maneuver the vehicle from the sinkhole I'd created. If only I'd taken thirty seconds to listen to some instructions, we could have avoided the whole scenario. But my pride wouldn't let me.

Ah, pride.

It keeps us from asking for help, and it also deludes us into thinking that we are greater, smarter, and more capable than we really are. It even makes some people think they can manage heavy vehicles in deep mud. Worse than that, it tricks us into believing that we are the masters of our own destiny and that we can control what happens in our lives.

"Look at the proud! They trust in themselves, and their lives are crooked," God told Habakkuk. In one short statement God gives a cause (the proud trust in themselves) and its effect (their lives are crooked). He's saying something really important here that we need to pay attention to.

If we want to live with greatness and purpose, we can't do it with pride as our foundation.

We'll never get where we want to go, and our lives will be characterized by crooked chaos.

Pride leaves no room for God to work. It says, "I trust in my own ability to manage my life," which sounds uncannily like the psalmist's words: "In his pride the wicked man does not seek him; in all his thoughts there is no room for God" (Psalm 10:4, NIV).

In contrast, humility is an attitude that leaves plenty of space for God to be active, and that's just the way He wants it. It keeps us dependent on Him, looking to Him for our purpose, our direction, and our help. Humility causes us to readily admit our shortcomings and recognize our need for others.

Read almost any book on finding your purpose or discovering your destiny, and you'll find several concepts put forth, many of which center on your own achievements. A Google search can produce lists of characteristics that will help you achieve success, such as confidence, drive, perseverance, talent, excellence, people skills, organizational prowess, and even pride. Humility is rarely mentioned.

Perhaps it's because the search for meaning and purpose is often approached as a *self*-centered endeavor, with the end goal of personal satisfaction. Unfortunately, that line of thinking neglects one key factor: none of this life is even possible without God.

I believe Romans 11:36 puts things into perspective: "For everything comes from him and exists by his power and is intended for his glory. All glory to him forever! Amen." A humble heart is at the center of *what moves God toward us*. When we live humbly before

Him, something remarkable happens: He lifts us up to places of honor and influence. He showers us with His grace, and He gives us added wisdom.

As St. Augustine is quoted as saying, "Humility is the foundation of all other virtues." In God's world, purpose and calling go hand in hand—with humility.

READ

In the same way, you who are younger must accept the authority of the elders. And all of you, dress yourselves in humility as you relate to one another, for "God opposes the proud but gives grace to the humble." So humble yourselves under the mighty power of God, and at the right time he will lift you up in honor. Give all your worries and cares to God, for he cares about you.   I PETER 5:5-7

REFLECT

Humility asks us to acknowledge our imperfections. It requires that we admit when we are wrong and then change course. It counsels putting others first in thought, word, and deed, and it avoids the narcissistic self-promotion so rampant today.[12]   DAVID BOBB

Humility is not thinking less of yourself, it's thinking of yourself less.   ATTRIBUTED TO C. S. LEWIS

Do you struggle with humility? Join the crowd. Consider these ways to cultivate humility in your life:

- Live in gratitude.
- Recognize the greatness of God.

147

- Experience nature—the work of God.
- Focus on promoting others.

RESPOND

1. Ask someone for advice or help. Listen without having to one-up or get defensive.

2. Write one way you can compliment or credit another person at work or somewhere else. _____

   _____

   _____

   _____

3. List ten things you are grateful for today.

   1. _____

   2. _____

   3. _____

   4. _____

   5. _____

   6. _____

   7. _____

   8. _____

   9. _____

   10. _____

4. Go for a walk outside and pay special attention to the details of creation. Experience the bigness of creation and the

smallness of yourself. Write your thoughts about it on the lines provided. _____

_____

_____

_____

_____

_____

_____

Do a kind deed without anyone knowing it was you. Doesn't that make you feel amazing?

.... Day Three ....
LIVE RIGHTEOUSLY

. . . .

"But the righteous will live . . ."
HABAKKUK 2:4

"Is THERE ANYTHING you can do to help our friends?" My son-in-law's e-mail landed in my inbox early one Thursday morning. His message elaborated: A single mom, along with her three children, needed a place to stay for a couple of weeks while they were in between housing situations. The e-mail was sent to a list of his local contacts, so I knew there were many people considering the question.

I hesitated. A book deadline loomed in two weeks, and I was way behind schedule. If I focused on it with no distractions, I *might* be able to make it. I'm a creative soul who needs absolute quiet when I write, which normally works well in an "empty nest" house with no children or pets. I know myself well; if we were to invite a family in, I'd be tempted to play games and watch movies and make food . . . the last things I could afford to do, considering my time crunch. And yet . . .

"Did you see the e-mail?" Tom asked as he walked into the office.

"Yes. We have to invite them to stay here. It's the right thing to do," I replied. Our house was the closest to the kids' school and the mom's work, so it made the most sense.

We would make it work.

It's not every day that we are presented with a choice this big. Doing what's right more often shows up in much smaller, seemingly inconsequential scenarios. When I hear the word *righteous*, I tend to think of the slang definitions: "genuine, excellent." You know, what a surfer might call the perfect wave, or what I might say when I see a fair price on a mercury glass lamp with a burlap shade I need for my living room.

Righteous is a word that shows up over and over again in the Bible. It means "acting in accord with divine or moral law: free from guilt or sin." Merriam-Webster.com goes on to define it as "arising from an outraged sense of justice or morality."

The simplest way to think of it? Doing what is right.

> ## Righteousness—doing what's right— is what we are all called to do.

Years ago, when I was trying to figure out my purpose in life, I spent a lot of time honing my artistic skills and working on my creative abilities. I put myself into position for opportunities to use my gifts, and I took on the posture of readiness. I did all the things we've been talking about in our six weeks together. Unfortunately, my phone did not ring off the hook with churches or organizations needing my skill set. Nobody e-mailed me with a choice position in a high-visibility venue for my art. Puzzling, huh?

What did happen was pretty unglamorous. A local nonprofit needed occasional volunteers to help care for children. Not exactly what my "calling" was. But I was available, and they were short-handed. It seemed like the right thing to do, so I did it.

When I was given too much change at the grocery store, I gave it back.

When a homeless man approached me for a handout, I bought him a hamburger.

When my bills were due, I paid them.

When I was done with my shopping cart, I returned it to the corral.

None of these things were remotely artistic or creative, but all were part of my calling *to do what is right.*

Habakkuk 2:4 compares the crooked lives of the proud to the lives of the righteous. God is implying here that the righteous live in a straightforward manner. They are characterized by choosing morally right paths and being motivated by integrity. They do the right thing.

And when they do the right thing, the psalmist says they receive a promise from God.

> Surely, LORD, you bless the righteous;
> you surround them with your favor as with a shield.
>
> PSALM 5:12, NIV

Choosing to live righteously brings God's favor and blessing. And *out of* that blessing will flow a greater sense of God's purpose.

READ

> The LORD God is our sun and our shield.
> He gives us grace and glory.
> The LORD will withhold no good thing
> from those who do what is right.
>
> PSALM 84:11

O people, the LORD has told you what is good,
 and this is what he requires of you:
to do what is right, to love mercy,
 and to walk humbly with your God.

MICAH 6:8, EMPHASIS ADDED

REFLECT

What image comes to mind when you picture a "righteous" person?
Is it a positive or negative one? Why? _____

_____

_____

_____

_____

 Doing what's right is not only reactive but proactive. Often, we know
we should take a certain action but find reasons not to get involved or
go the extra mile. Rather than ignore the impulse, we should listen to
our conscience (which is one way God speaks to us) and do it.

 Doing what's right is about making fair decisions, looking out for
the welfare of others, obeying rules, and paying it forward.

 Righteousness is integrity in everyday clothing.

RESPOND

1. Pay it forward: Do a small act of kindness for someone without
expecting anything in return.

2. Finish these next two sentences.
An injustice that bothers me is _____

_____

_____

_____

I will take one action to combat this injustice: _____

_____

_____

_____

_____

Day Four
LIVE FAITHFULLY

". . . by their faithfulness to God."

HABAKKUK 2:4

HABAKKUK COULD NOT HAVE KNOWN how powerfully these words would echo through the millennia, into the world of the New Testament writers and beyond. This statement would even be responsible for sparking a great reformation of the church in the sixteenth century.

In essence, this verse is the very heart of both the Jewish and the Christian faiths.

While scholars may debate the translation of *faithfulness*, or *faith*, I'm reminded of the very real way God illuminates His truth in different times, to different people, in special ways. We live both *in faithfulness* to God and *by faith* in God. Both concepts are vital to understanding the way God works and how we are to live.

I'm inspired by the word *faithfulness*, especially as it relates to us in our arena of life purpose. Faithful living is steadfast, constant, and firm.

Faithfulness is being fully devoted to the value of the present moment for lasting, eternal purposes.

It embraces activities considered mundane as worthy of effort, service that is considered menial as meaningful, and situations that are difficult as glorious pursuits.

Faithfulness finds beauty in commitment.

An acquaintance of mine recently posted a photo of her parents on Facebook. Holding hands and smiling at one another like a couple of newlyweds, they were celebrating their *sixty-second* anniversary. Talk about beauty in commitment! Most people hope that they can experience such enduring love, but what trips many of us up is the sheer dailiness of what that kind of faithfulness is all about. There is not much glory in washing dishes or doing laundry for sixty-two years. Not a whole lot of accolades in putting the needs of another person first.

Faithfulness is all about doing the little things that matter.

You see, most of us are eager to get suited up for a hard-fought, glorious battle that will test our mettle and result in an amazing victory. But fewer of us are prepared to withstand the small, steady requirements of lasting love, or enduring faith, or hey, taking the trash out every Tuesday and Friday.

Faithfulness embraces the fact that living out our life purpose may look a lot like, well, work. When you are willing to do the small tasks without looking for reward or acclaim, God will reward you with greater things.

READ

If you are faithful in little things, you will be faithful in large ones. But if you are dishonest in little things, you won't be honest with greater responsibilities.   LUKE 16:10

REFLECT

Character, which God wants us to develop for His purposes, is being formed through faithfulness in small things. Here are a few great quotes that touch on that very idea:

A little thing is a little thing, but faithfulness in little things is a great thing.   JAMES HUDSON TAYLOR

Be faithful in small things because it is in them that your strength lies.   MOTHER TERESA

The goal of faithfulness is not that we will do work for God, but that He will be free to do His work through us. God calls us to His service and places tremendous responsibilities on us. He expects no complaining on our part and offers no explanation on His part. God wants to use us as He used His own Son.   OSWALD CHAMBERS, *My Utmost for His Highest*

RESPOND

Be fully present in each activity today, no matter how mundane it is.

1. List three "requirements" of your day that you find unfulfilling, repetitive, or mundane. _____
   _____
   _____

_____

_____

_____

_____

2. As you do these tasks, imagine that each one is being done *for God*. Pay attention to the details—the sights, the sounds, your feelings—being mindful of each moment. Write your experience on the lines provided: _____

_____

_____

_____

_____

_____

3. How does the idea of faithfulness change how you view your "have-to" list of activities? _____

_____

_____

_____

_____

_____

Day Five
LIVE WORSHIPFULLY

*"I have heard all about you, LORD.
I am filled with awe by your amazing works."*

HABAKKUK 3:2

RIGHTEOUSNESS AND FAITHFULNESS, which we discussed in the two previous days, might sound an awful lot like wearisome deeds done in dutiful resignation. I can just see it: shoulders slumped, feet shuffling away, you go and obey some long, involved command from on high.

I mean, that's how *I* sometimes do righteousness and faithfulness. Not exactly the picture of enthusiastic, wholehearted obedience. Good thing there is a way to light these two on fire! Let me explain.

Several years ago, a church we attended experienced a difficult transition. People lined up on different sides of one issue in heated debates over the "right" and the "wrong" way to go. A special committee was formed. Meetings were called. Members called the pastor on the phone. People discussed it in Sunday school.

The issue wasn't about choosing a new pastor, or building a new wing for the youth. It wasn't over how money should be spent.

It was over music.

Worship style.

Everyone had his or her preference: traditional hymns or contemporary choruses. Drums or no drums. Organ or electric guitar. Hands down in reverent prayer or hands raised in adoration. Some people left the church because the Sunday morning music wasn't their style. Others sat in the back row of pews with arms crossed. Still others thought the music was just perfect the way it was.

We all got caught up in thinking that worship was all about the music on Sunday mornings. In reality, worship is about so much more.

Worship is actually a whole *lifestyle*—or at least it should be. It encompasses every decision, every action, and every thought. It is a life that says to God, "This is *all* for you."

Worship turns righteousness and faithfulness into a dance of gratitude.

It turns our slumped shoulders and shuffling steps of servitude into a ballet of joyful significance. We can exult in daily graces, and even difficulties, because of the beauty of God's presence within every moment.

Habakkuk devoted one-third of his book to worship. He knew that hard times were ahead for him and his people, and yet his soul longed to connect with God by remembering His greatness and awesomeness. He chose to rejoice in the midst of his journey, and in so doing, he found strength to answer his calling as a prophet and poet.

Worship gives meaning to our quest to live out our dreams and passions because we don't seek them simply for our own sake. We pursue them in order to fully embrace all that we are created to be—for *God's* glory. Living in worship brings everything into proper perspective: all our hopes and dreams, our work and efforts, our thoughts and goals—they are all for Him. Giving it all back to our Creator opens the doors for His Spirit to work within us.

"Thou hast formed us for Thyself," St. Augustine said to God, "and our hearts are restless till they find rest in Thee."[13]

Worship is the rest our souls find in God. When we realize that "everything comes from him and exists by his power and is intended for his glory" (Romans 11:36), we can drink deeply of His presence and allow ourselves to be vessels—conduits—of His grace to the world.

Whatever we do—in big and small ways—His purposes are being accomplished through us.

READ

Even though the fig trees have no blossoms,
and there are no grapes on the vines;
even though the olive crop fails,
and the fields lie empty and barren;
even though the flocks die in the fields,
and the cattle barns are empty,
yet I will rejoice in the LORD!
I will be joyful in the God of my salvation!
The Sovereign LORD is my strength!
He makes me as surefooted as a deer,
able to tread upon the heights.

HABAKKUK 3:17-19

REFLECT

The time is coming—indeed it's here now—when true worshipers will worship the Father in spirit and in truth. The Father is looking for those who will worship him that way.

JOHN 4:23

Whom have I in heaven but you?
    I desire you more than anything on earth.
My health may fail, and my spirit may grow weak,
    but God remains the strength of my heart;
    he is mine forever.

PSALM 73:25-26

Man's chief end is to glorify God, and to enjoy him forever.

WESTMINSTER SHORTER CATECHISM

RESPOND

Is your life characterized by worship?

Here are some ways to embrace a lifestyle of worship:

- Start the day with gratitude. Give thanks for three things before you get out of bed.
- Be mindful of God's presence in each moment.
- Sing. "Break out in praise," says Psalm 98:4.
- Acknowledge God's handiwork in creation. Notice every astounding detail in the world around you.
- Spend time learning about who God is and getting to know Him more.
- Give of your time, money, and resources.
- Love others.
- Live aware of your need for not only God's *saving* grace but also His *daily* grace.
- Let righteousness, faithfulness, and humility be a vehicle for worship.
- See your passion and purpose as your unique way of giving God glory.

First Corinthians 10:31 sums it up well:

Whether you eat or drink, or whatever you do, do it all for the glory of God.

Dear God, thank You for Your work in my life. I give all I have back to You: my gifts, abilities, talents, and skills . . . as well as my weaknesses, failures, experiences in the past, and even my uncertainties about the future. I ask that You would take all of it and use it for Your glory. I offer it as an expression of worship to You. I know that You delight in creating beautiful things and causing Your purposes to be fulfilled in this world, and I give thanks that I get to participate in what You are doing. Thank You for guiding me in good paths, for helping me to see Your will clearly, and for keeping Your hand upon me at all times. I can trust that You will be faithful to Your promises and that You will never leave me on my own. Keep showing me how I can use my passions and dreams for Your glory! It is with great joy and gratitude that I live in worship to You . . . with all I am and ever will be. Amen.

ACKNOWLEDGMENTS

A special thanks to the team at Tyndale House Publishers: to Sarah Atkinson, who believed I'd have something to say on finding your purpose; to Bonne Steffen, editor extraordinaire, for taking my manuscript and making it readable and engaging; and to Jennifer Phelps, whose design made it all look pretty.

Thank you to Leslie Nunn Reed and Susan Ellingburg with the BELONG Tour, who have a heart for women everywhere. It's a privilege to be part of your vision.

And thank you to my husband, Tom. He always encourages me to live my purpose, and regularly picks up the slack when that purpose lops over and makes me forget about eating, sleeping, and—I don't know—laundry.

ABOUT THE AUTHOR

RACHEL ANNE RIDGE is the author of the popular book *Flash*, as well as a professional artist and designer. Rachel blogs at *Home Sanctuary*, where since 2006 she has encouraged women to find joy in their journeys and daily lives. She has also served as a writer for Going Beyond Ministries with Priscilla Shirer. Rachel is wife to Tom, mom to three grown children, and Nona to four littles. The Ridges live in Texas.

ENDNOTES

1. Mary DeMuth, *The Wall Around Your Heart* (Nashville: Thomas Nelson, 2013), 15.
2. Matthew Kelly, *The Rhythm of Life* (New York: Simon & Schuster, 2004), 260–262.
3. Eleanor Roosevelt, *You Learn by Living* (New York: Harper & Row, 1960), 29–30.
4. Todd Kashdan, "The Power of Curiosity," *Experience Life*, May 2010, https://experiencelife.com/article/the-power-of-curiosity/.
5. The earliest known attribution of a version of this quote to Twain occurred in 1907 in an advertisement in the magazine *Outing: Sport, Adventure, Travel, Fiction* (volume 50). However, credit for this saying should go to the controversial novelist and essayist Grant Allen, who published a variant of it in 1894, then restated it within at least three of his novels.
6. Here are just a few samples of studies that confirm this: Steve Crabtree, "Social Satisfaction Linked to Health Satisfaction Worldwide," Gallup website, February 17, 2012, http://www.gallup.com/poll/152738/Social-Support-Linked-Health-Satisfaction-Worldwide.aspx; Julianne Holt-Lunstad, Timothy B. Smith, and J. Bradley Layton, "Social Relationships and Mortality Risk: A Meta-analytic Review," PLOS Medicine website, July 27, 2010, http://journals.plos.org/plosmedicine/article?id=10.1371/journal.pmed.1000316#s3; and "Loneliness, Like Chronic Stress, Taxes the Immune System," The Ohio State University website, January 19, 2013, http://researchnews.osu.edu/archive/lonely.htm.
7. Dale Carnegie, *How to Win Friends and Influence People* (New York: Simon & Schuster, 1981), 52.
8. C. S. Lewis, "Hamlet: The Prince or the Poem?" in *Selected Literary Essays* (Cambridge University Press, 2003), 99.
9. See Michael Hyatt, "5 Reasons Why You Should Commit Your Goals to Writing," https://michaelhyatt.com/5-reasons-why-you-should-commit-your-goals-to-writing.html.
10. See "Smart Goal Setting," Smart Goals Guide website, http://www.smart-goals-guide.com/smart-goal-setting.html. I have adapted the acronym for my chart.
11. For a summary of the study, see "Dominican Research Cited in Forbes Article," Dominican University of California website, accessed April 8, 2016, http://www.dominican.edu/dominicannews/dominican-research-cited-in-forbes-article.
12. See David J. Bobb, "Benjamin Franklin, George Washington, and the Power of Humility in Leadership," Fast Company website, September 27, 2013, http://www.fastcompany.com/3018516/leadership-now/benjamin-franklin-george-washington-and-the-power-of-humility-in-leadership. Bobb is the author of *Humility: An Unlikely Biography of America's Greatest Virtue* (Nashville: Thomas Nelson, 2013).
13. *The Confessions of St. Augustine.* See http://www.leaderu.com/cyber/books/augconfessions/bk1.html.

NOTES

The heartwarming true tale of an irrepressible donkey who needed a home —and forever changed a family.

978-1-4143-9783-2 (Hardcover)
978-1-4143-9784-9 (Softcover)

When Rachel Anne Ridge discovered a wounded, frightened donkey standing in her driveway, she couldn't turn him away. And against all odds, he turned out to be the very thing her family needed most. They let him into their hearts . . . and he taught them things they never knew about life, love, and faith.

Prepare to fall in love with Flash: a quirky, unlikely hero with gigantic ears, a deafening bray, a personality as big as Texas, and a story you'll never forget.

Available everywhere books are sold.

CP0850

YOU'RE INVITED

To be part of a community of real women who share their struggles and heartaches, hopes and dreams . . . a place where you can settle in and be accepted, just as you are. Join in through the resources below and at BELONGtour.com.

You Belong
An inspiring collection of reflections from a wide variety of women. Stories of identity, purpose, relationships, and living out your faith offer plenty of "me, too" moments. You'll laugh, wipe away an occasional tear, and gain fresh perspective.

Belonging Journal
A space to capture your thoughts, prayers, and dreams. Encouraging verses and insightful quotes from a wide-ranging group of women are sprinkled across lined pages, designed to motivate and inspire you to pour out your heart . . . and explore what it means to belong.

Made to Belong
Go on a six-week journey to discover and pursue your unique calling. In this study of Habakkuk, you'll dig deep, try new things, and step out of your comfort zones as you step into an exciting and fulfilling future.

Designed to Pray
This eight-week adventure is filled with activities—everything from coloring pages to writing prompts to doodling. Here you'll find space to let go of your fears and expectations and discover what it means to engage with the One who loves you.

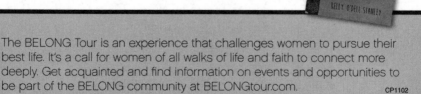

The BELONG Tour is an experience that challenges women to pursue their best life. It's a call for women of all walks of life and faith to connect more deeply. Get acquainted and find information on events and opportunities to be part of the BELONG community at BELONGtour.com.

CP1102

This is BIG.

Bigger than any one of us. *Because it's not about one of us; it's about all of us.*
When we gather, connect, and share, something happens. We change. We grow.
We want hearty exchanges with the people we love and safe places to fall.
We want to unpeel the layers and offer the best of ourselves.
Our best is rarely perfect, but that's OK.
We'll take real over perfect any day. And real happens here.

We have learned what it means to experience God's love in a real way
and renewed our belief in each other (and ourselves).

When we look at you, we see untapped power that can change the world.
Let's fan that flame and make things happen. We can do this. You are not alone.
We've readied a place for you to come in, to share, to heal, and to dance . . .

To BELONG.

JEN
hatmaker

ANGELA
davis

NICHOLE
nordeman

SHAUNA
niequist

SHARON
irving

PATSY
clairmont

At live events that bring women together in arenas across the country, remarkable
communicators gather with thousands of women to talk about how to live a fun,
faith-filled, purposeful life. There are plenty of personal stories, music, laughter, and
maybe even some tears in this Friday-night-to-Saturday event, where every woman
can find a place to belong.

**Get acquainted and find how you can be a part
of the BELONG community at BELONGtour.com.**

CP1103